Praise for *The Teaching Strategy Handbook*

The Teaching Strategy Handbook is an essential addition to every professional library and is perfect for any educator looking to refresh their craft. It serves as a practical and encouraging guide for simplifying methods that lead to student success and a more rewarding practice. Rather than promoting complex new systems, its greatest strength is the well-organized outline of a variety of strategies, many of which can be implemented immediately in your classroom.

—Christina Prince
Teacher of English for Speakers of Other Languages; Teacher of the Year
Waterway Elementary School
Little River, South Carolina

The Teaching Strategy Handbook exemplifies the art and science of teaching in action. Drawing from years of expertise across diverse classrooms and educational leadership roles, the authors present practical solutions for challenges facing educators today—including engagement, inclusion, technology, and teacher well-being. Every educator can benefit from having this guide in their toolkit.

—Jannelle Kubinec
Chief Executive Officer, WestEd
San Francisco, California

Practical, empowering, and immediately usable, *The Teaching Strategy Handbook* is a must-have teaching strategy handbook. With clear, actionable steps teachers can easily implement, it also serves as a valuable tool for evaluators and instructional coaches. Addressing engagement, classroom management, academic learning gaps, family involvement, and teacher burnout, this book supports both student success and sustainable, high-quality teaching and instruction.

—Jenna Woodland, EdD
Superintendent, Evergreen Park Elementary School District
Evergreen Park, Illinois

What a goldmine of information is packed into *The Teaching Strategy Handbook*. This innovative book is brilliantly organized around major classroom challenges. Realizing that teaching is both science and art, the authors provide the research behind each strategy and then coach readers in how to best achieve individual goals. This book is your go-to guide in making you the teacher you always wanted to be.

—Laura Colker, EdD
Researcher, Trainer, and Author of *The Creative Curriculum for Preschool*
Washington, DC

The Teaching Strategy Handbook is a bit like a magic box. Once opened, it provides the essential tools to become a more dynamic teacher and to cultivate more engaged and successful students. Undoubtedly, it revitalizes our practice and offers new ways to create an authentic academic environment—one that is creative, relevant, inclusive, and enjoyable. I worked with two of the authors for years, and they have placed the best of their best classroom practices in this practical volume. This is a text every new teacher must have as a guide, and one that experienced educators can use as a valuable refresher for evolving pedagogical approaches.

—Magda Molina
Spanish Literature Teacher; Teacher of the Year
Nogales High School
Nogales, Arizona

A practical, research-informed lifeline for today's educators, *The Teaching Strategy Handbook* delivers more than 200 immediately usable solutions to real classroom challenges: engagement, behavior, learning gaps, inclusion, assessment, and teacher well-being. Organized for quick access and grounded in teacher-tested practice, this book respects educators' time while elevating their impact. It functions like having expert instructional coaches on call. It's clear, credible, and relentlessly useful.

—Vickie E. Lake, PhD
Associate Dean and Professor, The University of Oklahoma
Tulsa, Oklahoma

Thanks for this practical resource with 200+ actionable strategies to address our current instructional challenges. Grounded in current research, *The Teaching Strategy Handbook* emphasizes both explicit and inquiry-based instruction to support student engagement, well-being, and rigorous learning. A welcome addition to our PD collection, it's accessible across a spectrum of teacher experience and training and manages to recenter people, not technology, at the heart of education. A must-have!

—John McKeown, EdD
Literacy Coordinator, Üsküdar American Academy
Istanbul, Turkey

THE
TEACHING
STRATEGY
Handbook

Many ISTE+ASCD members received this book as
a member benefit upon its initial release.

Learn more at **iste-ascd.org/member-books**

Other ISTE+ASCD books by these authors:

The Instructional Coaching Handbook:
200+ Troubleshooting Strategies for Success
by A. Keith Young, Angela Bell Julien,
and Tamarra Osborne

Training Design, Delivery, and Diplomacy: An
Educator's Guide
by A. Keith Young and Tamarra Osborne

Confident Classroom Management Moves
(QuickWins! Strategy Cards)
by A. Keith Young

A. KEITH YOUNG | ANGELA BELL JULIEN
TAMARRA OSBORNE | JUDITH MENDOZA-JIMÉNEZ

THE
TEACHING
STRATEGY
Handbook

200+ SOLUTIONS FOR COMMON
CLASSROOM CHALLENGES

iste+ascd

Arlington, Virginia USA

iste+ascd

2111 Wilson Boulevard, Suite 300 • Arlington, VA 22201 USA
Phone: 800-933-2723 or 703-578-9600
Website: iste-ascd.org • Email: memsupport@iste-ascd.org
Author guidelines: ascd.org/write

Richard Culatta, *Chief Executive Officer;* Genny Ostertag, *Managing Director, Book Acqui-sitions & Editing;* Stephanie Bize, *Acquisitions Editor;* Mary Beth Nielsen, *Director, Book Editing & Design;* Jamie Greene, *Senior Editor;* Lisa Hill, *Graphic Designer;* Valerie Younkin, *Senior Production Designer;* Emily Reed, *Senior Director, Publishing Operations;* Kelly Marshall, *Production Manager;* Shajuan Martin, *E-Publishing Specialist*

PAPERBACK ISBN: 978-1-4166-3430-0   ASCD product #126014   m4/26
PDF EBOOK ISBN: 978-1-4166-3431-7; see Books in Print for other formats.
Quantity discounts are available: email programteam@ascd.org or call 800-933-2723, ext. 5773, or 703-575-5773. For desk copies, go to www.ascd.org/deskcopy.

ISTE+ASCD Member Book No. FY26-3. ISTE+ASCD mails member books quarterly (Jan–Mar, Apr–Jun, Jul–Sep, Oct–Dec) with 4 books to Enhanced members and 8 books to Pro members. For current details on membership, see iste-ascd.org/member-books.

Library of Congress Cataloging-in-Publication Data is available for this title.
Names: Young, A. Keith author | Julien, Angela Bell author | Osborne, Tamarra author | Mendoza-Jimenez, Judith author
Title: The teaching strategy handbook : 200+ solutions for common classroom challenges / A. Keith Young, Angela Bell Julien, Tamarra Osborne, Judith Mendoza-Jimenez.
Description: Arlington, Virginia USA : ISTE+ASCD, [2026] | Includes bibliographical refer-ences and index.
Identifiers: LCCN 2026000714 (print) | LCCN 2026000715 (ebook) | ISBN 9781416634300 paperback | ISBN 9781416634317 pdf
Subjects: LCSH: Effective teaching | Classroom environment | Motivation in education
Classification: LCC LB1025.3 .Y63 2026 (print) | LCC LB1025.3 (ebook)
LC record available at https://lccn.loc.gov/2026000714
LC ebook record available at https://lccn.loc.gov/2026000715

35 34 33 32 31 30 29 28 27 26   1 2 3 4 5 6 7 8 9 10 11 12

This book is dedicated to our husbands—
our quiet anchors and steadfast companions.
Thank you for the steady love, laughter, and patience
that carried us through long writing nights and
countless edits. Your faith in our work has been a
constant source of strength and joy for us.

Márcio F. Almeida
Paul Julien
Nathaniel Osborne
David A. Jiménez

THE TEACHING STRATEGY Handbook

Introduction

Teaching today is no small feat. Each day brings new hurdles—whether it's addressing behavioral challenges, motivating disengaged students, navigating the lingering impacts of pandemic recovery, or managing the inevitable curveballs involved with integrating new technology. Recognizing this, we've designed this hands-on, practical guide to target the ten more prevalent classroom challenges teachers face. Readers will find more than 200 actionable ideas and solutions teachers are already successfully using, organized using recent findings and issue maps from trusted organizations such as Educators for Excellence (2024), Pew Research Center (2023, 2024), and RAND (2024). Whether the goal is to boost student engagement, master classroom management, or adapt lessons for diverse learners, we've gathered strategies rooted in the newest studies and insights. Each chapter includes examples from teachers across the United States, vividly illustrating how these techniques come to life and helping educators envision practical ways to implement them effectively in their classrooms.

We understand that time is precious. It isn't necessary to read every page. Instead, simply locate a current classroom challenge in the table of contents, jump directly to that chapter, and start experimenting with strategies for your classroom. In short, feel free to dip into chapters in any order that works best. Each chapter features clearly numbered tactics alongside authentic, teacher-tested examples. Where applicable, we explicitly highlight a strategy's effectiveness according to research, especially John Hattie's (2023, 2024) updated effect sizes, so a teacher can quickly pinpoint methods likely to yield strong academic outcomes—for example, "effect size = 0.40 (Hattie, 2023)."

Although we're huge fans of Hattie's visible learning findings, we've intentionally included some strategies that show lower effect sizes because they target valuable educational outcomes beyond standardized academic achievement. A few of these suggestions include increased student enjoyment, improved classroom culture, stronger family-school connections, meaningful social-emotional development, greater student agency, and specialized support that addresses specific learners' needs. These outcomes are significant whether they translate directly into immediate academic gains on standardized measures or not.

To make it even easier to find a starting point, we've grouped strategies into three categories based on the level of preparation and effort involved:

 Immediate, low-prep strategies require little to no advance planning and can often be tried the same day.

 Routine, moderate-prep strategies involve a bit more setup but can be incorporated into your regular teaching flow with minimal disruption.

 **Long-term, high-prep strategies** take more time and planning but are designed to support lasting change.

These categories should help teachers choose strategies that fit their current capacity and take action without feeling overwhelmed.

Chapter 1: Student Engagement. Keeping students motivated and engaged remains challenging across all grades, subjects, and student groups. Surveys consistently show that disrupted learning environments and lingering emotional impacts have led many students to struggle both academically and socially (Canvas Study, 2022; Educators for Excellence, 2024; Pew Research Center, 2023). Although schools increasingly adopt affective education programs to enhance student engagement, consistently and effectively implementing these programs remains challenging (Skoog-Hoffman et al., 2024). Additional research reveals declines in student motivation in both online and in-person educational settings, highlighting the need for classroom strategies that promote a sense of belonging, personal responsibility, and intrinsic motivation (Hari Rajan et al., 2024). Jump into Chapter 1 to explore strategies that help reignite students' enthusiasm for learning and foster and sustain their motivation.

Chapter 2: Classroom Management: Affective Learning Gaps. Teachers frequently encounter challenges in managing student behavior and addressing mental health concerns, such as hyperactivity, defiance, anxiety, and stress (Educators for Excellence, 2024; Pew Research Center, 2024). Student misbehavior increasingly contributes to teacher burnout, disrupting learning environments significantly (Doan et al., 2024). Researchers emphasize the need to prioritize student self-regulation and emotional health since many students struggle with emotional management and sustained classroom engagement (Educators for Excellence, 2024; Pew Research Center, 2023). To this end, it's critical to implement affective education tactics that foster emotional regulation, coping mechanisms, and relationship-building skills to minimize classroom disruptions and create supportive learning environments (RAND, 2024; Skoog-Hoffman et al., 2024). Go directly to Chapter 2 for actionable ways to build emotionally supportive classrooms and effectively manage complex behaviors.

Chapter 3: Academic Learning Gaps. Addressing fundamental knowledge gaps remains paramount in today's classrooms. Educators should use targeted interventions and continuous progress tracking in class and during additional instructional time, such as tutoring or enrichment activities (National Center for Education

Statistics [NCES], 2023; Pew Research Center, 2023). Diagnostic and formative assessment is critical to identify individual student needs for tailored instructional responses (NCES, 2023). Consequently, schools nationwide are integrating social-emotional learning (SEL) into academic recovery initiatives to improve student achievement and overall well-being (RAND, 2024; Skoog-Hoffman et al., 2024). Dive into Chapter 3 now for practical strategies that pinpoint learning gaps and accelerate students' academic recovery.

Chapter 4: Special Needs in the General Ed Classroom. Meeting the diverse and complex needs of students who require individualized instruction continues to challenge and exhaust educators. Differentiated strategies help address these demands, fostering inclusive education for all learners (Canvas Study, 2022; Educators for Excellence, 2024), and research consistently highlights the importance of personalized learning plans and targeted interventions that support students with disabilities and multilingual learners (RAND, 2024). Turn to Chapter 4 now for practical, proven strategies that effectively support special education and multilingual students.

Chapter 5: Technology Integration. Seamless integration and management of technology is both essential and challenging in today's classrooms. Many of the teachers with whom we work often grapple with balancing technology-driven activities and traditional instructional approaches, seeking professional development to bolster their digital skills (Canvas Study, 2022; Pew Research Center, 2024; RAND, 2024). To address this, schools must invest in teacher training programs that maximize technology's role in personalized instruction, targeted intervention, and student engagement (Skoog-Hoffman et al., 2024). Explore Chapter 5 for tips from teachers on how best to integrate technology into instruction and unlock new possibilities for student engagement.

Chapter 6: Family Involvement. Parental involvement can significantly influence student performance. Research consistently demonstrates improved outcomes with balanced parental engagement, yet achieving this balance remains difficult for many educators (Pew Research Center, 2024). Strategies that foster meaningful relationships with parents and resources to help parents support their children's education are increasingly critical (Borrello, 2023; Educators for Excellence, 2024; RAND, 2024). Check out Chapter 6 for effective ways to build stronger parent partnerships and elevate student success.

Chapter 7: Assessment and Grading. Jump to Chapter 7 to discover innovative assessment and grading methods that improve fairness and drive student achievement. Educators are increasingly rethinking traditional grading methods to address learning gaps, implement formative assessment, and employ flexible, competency-based approaches to personalize learning and maintain high academic standards (Canvas Study, 2022; NCES, 2023; RAND, 2024).

Chapter 8: Teacher Burnout and Stress. Teacher stress and burnout have reached unprecedented levels, making professional support more vital than ever. Schools can enhance teacher support through mentorship programs, mental health resources, effective communication strategies, and collaborative opportunities (Educators for Excellence, 2024; RAND, 2024; Waterson, 2024). Turn to Chapter 8 to find practical strategies for managing stress, preventing burnout, and nurturing your professional well-being.

Chapter 9: Cultural Competency, Inclusivity, and Equity. Developing culturally competent, inclusive, and equitable teaching practices is more critical than ever. With this in mind, many schools have been actively rolling out professional development that emphasizes equity and inclusivity, fosters supportive and respectful learning environments, and employs culturally responsive teaching methods (Canvas Study, 2022; Educators for Excellence, 2024; RAND, 2024).

Explore Chapter 9 to strengthen your culturally responsive practices and create a more inclusive, equitable classroom.

Chapter 10: Take Action. We know that implementing new teaching and learning strategies can be daunting, so we've provided practical tips and actionable advice to seamlessly incorporate fresh ideas into daily classroom routines. Turn to Chapter 10 for teacher-tested tips that turn the strategies you've discovered in previous chapters into lasting instructional habits.

We—Keith, Tamarra, Angela, and Judith—are four passionate practitioners who live and breathe education every day. Among the four of us, we've worked broadly in education, teaching in diverse classrooms, leading schools, coaching educators from preschool to high school, and guiding instructional practices across districts around the globe. We don't just write about education; we're right there in the trenches, sleeves rolled up, working side by side with teachers, modeling lessons and coaching teachers and students on a weekly basis.

Leaders instantly connect with Keith's accessible coaching style, which is shaped by years of turning around schools in diverse communities from Puerto Rico to Arizona. Tamarra's expertise is in early childhood innovation. Her passion for nurturing young learners and her work at the nonprofit WestEd have transformed how early childhood educators assess and educate our youngest students. Angela spent decades refining instructional improvement methods and building meaningful relationships, ensuring every student has a path to success beyond high school. Judith's journey as an immigrant and bilingual special education advocate deeply informs her leadership as she passionately builds equitable, supportive programs that honor every student's unique story.

Our collective experience has taught us that teaching is both a science and an art that is challenging, dynamic, and deeply rewarding. In this book, we've distilled decades of real-world insights into actionable, practical strategies teachers can apply immediately.

Think of it as having four seasoned coaches in your corner, cheering you on, offering advice, and helping navigate the highs and lows of teaching today.

So jump in, find strategies that resonate with you and your students, and get ready to see your teaching journey transform. We're thrilled you're on this exciting adventure!

1

Student Engagement

Every classroom has students who struggle to stay focused. It doesn't matter if it's 1st grade or senior year of high school; teachers everywhere deal with kids who tune out, lose interest in lessons, or have trouble connecting meaningfully with classmates. Sound familiar? This chapter offers creative, straightforward ways to energize the classroom and draw students into the learning process. From quick warm-up activities that spark curiosity, to peer coaching approaches that build meaningful connections, to flexible grouping techniques that keep engagement high, these strategies will help boost students' enthusiasm and encourage both academic growth and emotional well-being.

This chapter bursts with more than 90 classroom-tested moves—fresh, flexible ways to spark curiosity, sustain attention, and turn passive learners into eager participants. Still need more ideas? Check out Chapters 3 and 4 for even more tips on getting (and keeping!) students plugged in and excited about learning.

Immediate, Low-Prep Strategies

Start with a Warm-Up

Begin lessons with engaging activities to capture attention. The human brain responds best to new learning when it can associate that learning with something fun or familiar. A "warm-up" should do just that. Think of it like a warm-up people do before starting a strenuous physical activity. They stretch and prepare their muscles for exercise, right? Why not do the same thing before "working out" the brain?

Often, we see warm-up activities that actually cool down students' desire to learn: they are silent, individual, and quiz-like. Effective warm-ups should energize students' brains. For example, present a higher-level thinking question from the previous day's learning and ask students to talk about what they think or remember that helps them answer the question. Ask them to discuss the question with a partner before writing a response in a daily calendar or warm-up journal. Have them refer to a text or their notes to support their thoughts and then share their justification with their partner or the class.

Engaging in a "mix and mingle" activity enriches students' thinking about previous learning and prepares them to learn new skills and information. In a 5th grade classroom in Hawaii, students begin each day with a question about what they learned the previous day. They then move along to music as they participate in a "stand up, pair up, hand up" activity—a quick, movement-based partner activity where students get up, find a classmate, and share responses or ideas to warm up their thinking and build connections. This activity warms up their brains and builds warm relationships among students.

Provide the Goal and Purpose

Imagine walking into a kitchen where a chef hands you random ingredients—flour, eggs, salt, chocolate chips—but does not explain what you're making. You might start mixing and simply guess how much to add (and when), but without a standard recipe or goal, you won't know if you're making cookies, a cake, or some type of paste for a science project. Teaching without explicitly stating the goal and reasoning behind each lesson is just like that. Students may go through the motions but will not understand how the pieces fit together or why they matter. Learning accelerates when students see how each concept builds toward mastery (Biggs et al., 2022; Hattie, 2023; Saphier et al., 2025), just as baking is more successful when the cook knows what they're making before they start.

One K–8 Arizona school embraced the need for students to see and hear the purpose and reason for each lesson. When the effort began, scores were quite low across the school. After a concerted effort by all teachers to post explicit objectives and provide students with statements of relevancy for their learning, the school made quick, significant student academic progress in one school year. Indeed, Hattie's *Visible Learning: The Sequel* (2023) reinforces this point: students learn best when they see the coherence between what they have already learned, what they are learning now, and what comes next.

An explicit goal and purpose for the lesson are foundational to "teacher clarity" (effect size = 0.85; Hattie, 2023), one of the most substantial influences on student achievement. Rather than forcing a contrived real-world connection, consider helping students actively construct meaning from their learning objectives. One practical method is to have students conduct a "vocabulary search" within the lesson's standard before instruction begins. By discussing what new words might mean and predicting what they will learn, students uncover gaps in their knowledge and create a road map for what they need to understand. The teacher then listens, clarifies, and helps refine learning objectives in real time, making every student feel like an active participant rather than a passive recipient of information.

Likewise, when teachers are assigning group tasks or projects, they need to ensure the goals are clear and explicit. With older students, encourage them to ask clarifying questions such as "What is the main goal of this task?" "How will we measure our success?" and "Are we supposed to generate new ideas or evaluate existing ones?" When a teacher makes it a habit to clarify the goals, students focus their efforts appropriately and work more effectively as a team. This also improves their collaboration skills and enhances their overall learning outcomes by ensuring each group activity has a well-defined purpose.

Purpose-driven instruction isn't just about stating a standard; it's about making learning feel like a meaningful, step-by-step process toward a clear goal. So, before starting a lesson, think, "Would I want to cook a dish if I had no idea what it was supposed to become?" If not, then don't expect students to want to learn that way, either.

Share Success Stories to Motivate Learning

Sharing success stories motivates and inspires students. Using those stories will help students stay motivated as they learn. For example, the teacher might talk about how previous students used the writing skills they are learning to write letters for scholarships and jobs or tell younger students stories about how the math they are learning will help them in the next grade level: "Students who are able to divide whole numbers successfully are doing science experiments that require an understanding of fractions." To keep students engaged and progressing with a project, one middle school teacher relayed a story about a previous year when a diligent group of students was invited to the state capital to display what they had created and talk about their work. Make the classroom a place where students consistently hear about the bright futures they have ahead of them—and how those possibilities are related to their current learning goals.

Provide Whisper Feedback Regularly

Offering immediate, subtle feedback during lessons is powerful. When moving around the classroom, try to make it a "wondering" experience rather than just a "wandering" one. Wonder how each student is doing. Stop frequently to provide subtle, immediate feedback to students as they work. Use gentle nudges or whispers to guide them in the right direction without interrupting their focus. For example, if a student struggles with a math problem, quietly suggest a different approach or ask a guiding question such as "Tell me what you have thought about so far." Whisper a response that encourages students to move forward confidently and successfully.

This discreet feedback helps students stay on track and develop their problem-solving skills without feeling singled out or embarrassed. Providing immediate, subtle feedback also helps scaffold students' responses to higher-order questions, supporting their ability to answer more complex queries. Explicit feedback provides a marked impact on student achievement (effect size = 0.51; Hattie, 2023).

Teach Effective Time Management

Students of all ages need to learn to use time wisely. Something as simple as timers helps with students of all ages. They keep both students and the teacher on pace. Incorporating timers into lessons is an easy way to make strides and can be a powerful tool for enhancing student engagement, learning, personal efficiency, and lesson delivery. Here are a couple ways to use timers during lessons:

- Use a timer to track how much time is spent in teacher talk (e.g., giving directions and providing instructions) versus how much time students speak and engage in tasks. This can help find a balance that maximizes student participation, interaction, and teacher input.
- Set individual timers for students to help them stay focused and engaged in their work. This action can benefit students who struggle with attention and time management.

Even if this tactic initially feels uncomfortable, commit to trying it about a half-dozen times before deciding its effectiveness. Note whether this practice helps increase student learning, engagement, and efficiency in your lesson. By experimenting with this strategy, the teacher can gain insights into how time management affects the overall classroom dynamic—and then adjust their practices to support students' needs better.

Use Alternatives to Calling on One Student at a Time

The following are some tactics designed to involve more students when tempted to call on one student to answer a question in front of the class or complete a problem on the classroom whiteboard. Ideally, we want to engage all students at the same time instead of having most students sit silently while one performs for the entire class. This approach is an example of active participation, a principle of learning that increases students' rate and retention of learning (Saphier et al., 2025).

- **Flash Card Consensus.** Students simultaneously display prepared response cards (e.g., Agree/Disagree, A/B/C/D, True/False) to answer a question, enabling real-time assessment of class understanding.
- **Silent Signals.** Instead of verbal responses, students use predetermined hand gestures to express agreement, uncertainty, or a request for clarification, fostering immediate nonverbal feedback.
- **Write & Reveal.** Students record their responses on paper, in journals, or on sticky notes before discussing them with a partner or posting them for class analysis. This ensures every student contributes without requiring them to speak aloud.
- **Walk & Vote.** Post different possible answers to questions (e.g., vocabulary words, historical events, math solutions) throughout the classroom. Students physically walk to their chosen answer and discuss their reasoning within a group of like-minded students before sharing insights with the class.
- **Collaborative Rotation Writing.** Students write their initial thoughts on a large individual sheet of paper. After a set time, they rotate to another student's paper, where they add reflections, alternative perspectives, or supporting details.
- **Public Thought Wall.** Students write short responses on a communal space (e.g., chalkboard, whiteboard, digital

wall). The whole class then reviews and discusses diverse perspectives.

- **Reflect, Discuss, Report.** Students first process a question independently, then discuss it with a partner, and finally summarize key takeaways for and report to the larger group.
- **Dialogue Carousel.** Two concentric circles of students face each other and engage in short discussions. After each exchange, the outer circle rotates and the process is repeated, ensuring multiple perspectives are shared.
- **Reciprocal Teaching.** In small groups, students lead discussions, summarize key concepts, and question their peers. This encourages active participation and deeper comprehension of the text or content.
- **Anonymous Idea Bank.** Students jot down responses or solutions anonymously on slips of paper, which are then shuffled and redistributed for peer review and discussion. This encourages participation from all students, including those who might be hesitant to speak up.
- **Interactive Journals.** Students use journals (print or digital) to maintain ongoing written conversations with the teacher or classmates, exchanging reflections, questions, and feedback over time, which also strengthens written communication skills.
- **Finger Snaps, Knuckle Taps, or Tongue Clicks.** Students snap their fingers, tap their knuckles on their desk, or click their tongues to indicate agreement, appreciation, or acknowledgment. These subtle cues allow for quick whole-class feedback for both teachers and students while keeping the classroom environment focused and encouraging.
- **Answer Wheels.** Students use handheld spinners with answer choices (e.g., A, B, C, D), and they simultaneously reveal their selected responses, ensuring active engagement from the entire class.

- **Step Up for Understanding.** Instead of raising their hands, students physically stand up or step forward if they relate to an idea, agree with a statement, or support an argument. This creates an immediate, visible representation of student engagement.
- **Collective Readiness Stand.** Before one student volunteers to share an answer, the entire class stands to indicate readiness. This fosters a sense of group responsibility for learning, maintains high engagement, and signals that everyone is ready to listen to the volunteer.

When the teacher wants to spotlight one student—whether it's to answer a question, share an idea, or model a solution—they can still keep the rest of the class actively engaged by using a quick "group alert." This simple move lets the whole class know they're still expected to participate while someone else is speaking. For example, say, "Listen to Maureen's answer. As she talks, jot down key words you hear, compare her thinking to yours, and note anything you had in common or that was different."

If the teacher forgets to give the group alert before calling on a student, no problem—they can just loop back after the student's response and say, "Write that answer down if you didn't already have it" or "Turn to a neighbor and explain what the last two students said in your own words." This quick strategy, first described by Kounin (1970) and advocated more recently by Hattie and Clark (2019), helps eliminate mental off-ramps during whole-class discussions (i.e., when students tune out because they're unaccountable while someone else is talking) and keeps everyone in the learning loop.

Highlight Circles of Influence

One way to keep students motivated is to help them recognize what's under their control. Instead of worrying about things they can't change, encourage them to focus on practical actions they can actually do. For example, if students are having trouble understanding what they read, guide them to practice useful habits, such as summarizing key ideas after each paragraph or stopping to ask questions about the text as they go.

By regularly noticing their improvement and the effectiveness of these strategies, students build confidence and stay more engaged with their learning. When students learn more about the principles of a growth mindset, it can significantly enhance their ability to focus on controllable aspects of life and work (Dweck, 2016). Help them identify something they know how to do well (e.g., sewing, riding a bike, playing a specific video game, putting together outfits, baking, playing basketball) and have them talk through the steps they use in their area of expertise. How can they use those skills in their learning? Figure 1.1 shows how one student applied the Circles of Influence, identifying what they could control, what they could influence, and what was beyond their control.

Routine, Moderate-Prep Strategies

Use Future Casting

If traditional instructional strategies aren't working for specific students, try future casting, which is a guided imagery strategy that involves visualizing a timeline to reach a goal and reflect on the forces that support and hinder progress toward that goal (Bocchino, 1999; Young et al., 2023). Students should describe their goals verbally, imagine achieving them, and think through the steps necessary to realize their vision. This process has the potential to shift students' perspective and inspire creative thinking by addressing core values and assumptions. In addition, future casting is associated with students' commitment to their goals (effect size = 0.44; Hattie, 2023).

Figure 1.1   Circles of Influence

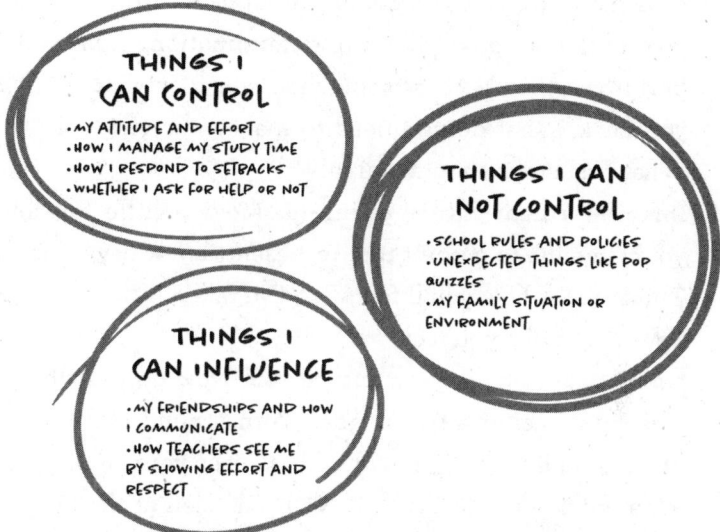

THINGS I
CAN CONTROL
• MY ATTITUDE AND EFFORT
• HOW I MANAGE MY STUDY TIME
• HOW I RESPOND TO SETBACKS
• WHETHER I ASK FOR HELP OR NOT

THINGS I CAN
NOT CONTROL
• SCHOOL RULES AND POLICIES
• UNEXPECTED THINGS LIKE POP
QUIZZES
• MY FAMILY SITUATION OR
ENVIRONMENT

THINGS I
CAN INFLUENCE
• MY FRIENDSHIPS AND HOW
I COMMUNICATE
• HOW TEACHERS SEE ME
BY SHOWING EFFORT AND
RESPECT

Source: Adapted from *The Instructional Coaching Handbook* (p. 14), by A. K. Young, A. B. Julien, and T. Osborne, 2023, ASCD.

Here are the steps students should follow when future casting:

1. **Choose a goal.** Think of an important goal you want to achieve, whether related to your schoolwork or social life. It should be significant and take a few weeks to achieve. You don't have to share it with anyone if you don't want to.

2. **Create a mental timeline.** Stand up and imagine a timeline stretching across the room. This timeline represents the time it will take to reach your goal.

3. **Visualize your achieved goal.** Walk to the end of your imagined timeline—to the point where you have achieved your goal. Step into this future success. Describe what it looks and sounds like. Imagine you're explaining it to someone else.

4. **Experience your vision.** Immerse yourself in your vision and describe what you feel and see. Picture yourself in this triumphant moment.

5. **Identify helpers and obstacles.** Go back to the start of your timeline. Look up the timeline and think about what will help you reach your goal (like your determination, skills, and support from others). At the same time, consider what might hold you back. What do you need to make your vision a reality? What first steps should you take?

6. **Imagine a near-future check-in.** Move a little forward on your timeline to a point that represents a few days from now. Think about how you'll feel if you've taken little action. How does that make you feel?

7. **Gain wisdom from your future self.** Now go past the point where you achieved your goal. Turn around and look back at the timeline. Imagine you are a wiser version of yourself. What advice would you give your past self at the beginning of the timeline? Write this advice down and use it to keep yourself motivated and to help you overcome obstacles as you work toward your goal.

Figure 1.2 visually maps the Future Casting process, showing how students move from imagining a goal to reflecting on the supports and obstacles along the path toward achieving it.

Implement Peer Coaching

Teachers can take specific steps to make peer coaching successful. Pair students to motivate and support one another. Peer coaching is a valuable tool as long as partners are genuinely coaching each other (and not just doing work for each other). Before beginning peer coaching, teach a lesson on asking reflective questions and encouraging others to continue their work. Give examples of what proper coaching looks like. All students should be part of the training. Once peer coaching time begins, carefully "wonder" around the room and listen to the conversations. Remind students, when necessary, of reflective questions. When done with fidelity, peer coaching can have a robust effect on learning (effect size = 0.55; Hattie, 2023).

During an observation of a peer coaching classroom, the observers heard a student being coached remind their coach, "Remember, you are supposed to ask me a question, not tell me exactly what to do." The coach smiled and thought momentarily before asking an insightful, reflective question. In an 8th grade English classroom, students were routinely placed in groups of three to act as authors, editors, and publishers for one another. The author presented their writing to the other two, the editor discussed language issues and sentence structure, and the publisher led a discussion about the content. The author took notes and summarized the changes they would make. Student writing scores soared in this classroom!

Figure 1.2   Future Casting Illustration

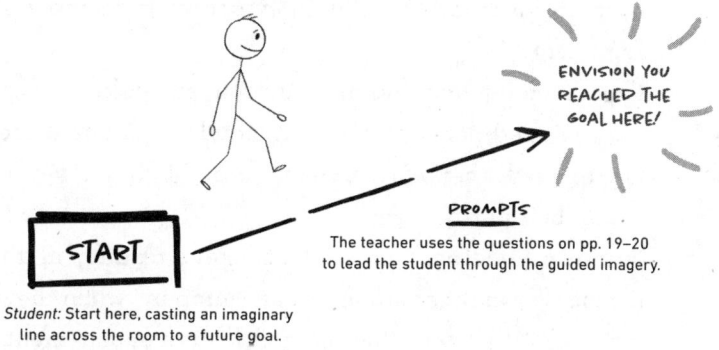

Student: Start here, casting an imaginary line across the room to a future goal.

Source: Adapted from *The Instructional Coaching Handbook* (p. 37), by A. K. Young, A. B. Julien, and T. Osborne, 2023, ASCD.

Boost Accountable Reading

When students actively engage in reading together, participation increases and provides a more dynamic and engaging alternative to having one student read at a time. A single student reading aloud often allows students prone to disengaging to drift away. Most strategies in this section involve peer reading, reading and writing, or verbal reading. Research shows that reading interactively—whether aloud to oneself, with a partner, or in a group—strengthens retention and deepens engagement (Watson & Busch, 2021). Additionally, reading strategies that involve peer interaction, discussion, text structure analysis, note taking, and written responses tend to result in higher levels of academic achievement (effect size = 0.47; Hattie, 2023).

To increase engagement and improve reading comprehension, integrate the following strategies, which are based on decades of literacy work and the research of Serravallo (2023) and others.

- **Interactive Reading**
  - › **Mark It Up.** Students actively engage with a text by circling, boxing, or underlining key elements. They respond to specific guidance, such as "Circle unfamiliar words, box in main ideas, and underline evidence that supports the argument."
  - › **Partner Relay Reading.** In pairs, students take turns reading assigned portions of a text aloud. If a student prefers not to read, they can summarize or highlight key ideas while their partner reads.
  - › **Jump-In Reading.** One student begins reading, and their partner (or another student) can "jump in" when they feel ready to take over. This method fosters engagement and keeps students actively listening.
  - › **Sticky Note Insights.** While reading, students jot down observations on sticky notes, using different colors to represent themes, patterns, or questions they have about the text.
  - › **Highlight & Reflect.** Students highlight key points as they read and write a one-sentence summary of each paragraph or section of text.

- **Purpose-Driven Reading**
  - > **Reading with a Goal.** Provide guiding questions to help students set a specific purpose or goal for reading. For example, "Read this passage to understand the author's perspective on climate change." After reading, students share their findings in pairs or small groups. This approach works well for listening and video-based materials as well.
  - > **Annotation Challenge.** Students interact with a text while reading using an annotation system (symbols, marginal notes, or a structured format).
  - > **Whisper Reading.** Students read aloud to themselves in a whisper. This method allows them to hear the words without disturbing others and reinforces fluency.

- **Collaborative and Performance-Based Reading**
  - > **Choral and Echo Reading.** The teacher reads a passage aloud, periodically pausing for the entire class to read together or repeat key portions. This technique helps reinforce vocabulary, model fluency, and improve comprehension. It is also particularly valuable when reading basic instructions (students are more likely to recall the instructions) or poetry (students are more likely to catch the beauty of the language).
  - > **Choice-Based Reading.** Students should be allowed to choose how they engage with a text, as long as there is visible interaction, such as reading aloud, annotating, or summarizing.
  - > **Walk & Read Conversations.** Assign students a passage to read and discuss while walking around the classroom. Research suggests light movement during learning can improve retention (Miller & Krizan, 2016).
  - > **Dramatic Roles.** When reading plays or scripted material, assign multiple groups instead of just one reader to each

role. Each group reads a single character's text, ensuring more students participate actively.

- **Scaffolded Reading**
  - > **Guided Choral Reading.** Students read a sentence and pause dramatically, prompting the class to continue reading aloud until the teacher takes over again. This technique promotes engagement and subtly prompts students to pay attention for the class's turn to read or stop reading.
  - > **Predictive Pattern Reading.** For repetitive texts, such as those with predictable phrasing, encourage students to join in reading the familiar segments. This interaction is particularly effective for early readers.
  - > **Peer Reading & Annotation.** In pairs, one student reads while the other jots down key information. They then swap roles, and a third student (if available) generates discussion questions based on the reading.

Implementing these strategies helps create a more interactive reading environment that improves comprehension, fosters collaboration, and builds student confidence in engaging with complex texts. Keith and Angela have even observed several university instructors deploy these strategies in college classrooms.

Foster Engagement with Various Media

Students can be motivated to engage in and respond to activities through tasks that require them to write, take notes, illustrate, or perform another interactive strategy. Many of the following tactics—which incorporate slide decks, lectures, videos, demonstrations, and listening activities—are adapted from Biggs and colleagues (2022) and Saphier and colleagues (2025).

- **Writing-Based Engagement**
  - > **Cornell Notes.** Students capture ideas on a page that is divided into sections: main ideas, key details, and a summary to process information (Pauk & Owens, 2013)
  - > **Guided Notes.** Fill in the blanks on a structured outline provided by the teacher.
  - > **Two-Column Notes.** Record main points on one side of a page and questions, reactions, or examples on the other.
  - > **Quick Writes.** Pause at key moments to jot down a summary or reaction in a minute or less.
  - > **Exit Tickets.** Summarize the most essential takeaways or pose a lingering question at the end of a lesson.
  - > **Learning Logs.** Write reflections on how new information connects to prior knowledge or experiences.
  - > **Key Sentence Capture.** Write down the essential sentence from each segment of a lecture or video.

- **Illustration and Concept Mapping Engagement**
  - > **Sketchnoting.** Use a combination of drawings, symbols, and words to visualize key ideas as notes.
  - > **Concept Mapping.** Create a web of related ideas, showing connections between and among concepts.
  - > **One-Pager Summaries.** Visually summarize key points on a single page, incorporating images, words, and symbols.
  - > **Storyboard Notes.** Draw a sequence of images to represent key points from a demonstration or lecture.
  - > **Timeline Sketching.** Draw a timeline to visually organize historical events or steps in a process.

- **Interactive and Kinesthetic Engagement**
  - > **Stop & Jot.** Pause and write down a key idea before moving forward.
  - > **Turn & Teach.** Verbally summarize new learning to a partner.

> **Annotation Challenge.** Use symbols (e.g., stars, question marks, emojis, exclamation points) to mark reactions in notes.
> **Color Coding.** Use different colors to highlight key terms, definitions, and supporting details.
> **Word Clouds.** Write the most important words about a topic in large letters and the supporting words, ideas, or concepts in a surrounding "cloud" of smaller letters.
> **Graphic Organizers.** Make simple, hand-drawn Venn diagrams, T-charts, tables, or flowcharts to capture key concepts.

- **Listening and Questioning Engagement**
  > **Think-Pair-Share Notes.** Listen, write a summary, and then critique a partner's summary.
  > **Q&A Charting.** Write down questions while listening, then revisit them afterward to seek answers.
  > **3-2-1.** After a lesson, write down three key takeaways, two questions, and one connection to prior knowledge.
  > **Predictions & Confirmations.** Before listening, predict what you expect to learn. Afterward, confirm or revise your predictions.

Arrange Flexible Grouping

Rearrange groups to keep interpersonal dynamics fresh. Healthy, positive relationships in the classroom are key to productive student engagement. Rearrange often. One teacher Keith knows gives each student a colored card with a number, a shape, a letter, and an animal. Students frequently shift groups based on the features of their card. Cooperative learning (effect size = 0.40; Hattie, 2023) and small-group learning (effect size = 0.46; Hattie, 2023) are related to higher student academic learning, and flexible grouping relates to both of these concepts.

Encourage Equitable Class Discussions

Classroom discussions don't just happen; they're the result of intention. Start off by laying the groundwork. Get students thinking with a short writing activity to bring out their questions and curiosity. Then lay out simple, clear ground rules—things like listening with respect, giving everyone a chance to speak (or opt out), and making space for both honesty and kindness. These norms aren't just for show. Referring to them often guides the group. Bonus tip? Rotate in student facilitators to build ownership and leadership (Hammond, 2025; Young et al., 2023).

Once things are rolling, keep the conversation lively and inclusive. Try a "round of reactions" with hand signals or taps to let everyone weigh in without speaking. Mix in partner talks, group annotations, and quick writes to shift the energy and bring in more voices. Watch for subtle signals that might indicate students want to talk but are reluctant (e.g., biting lips, covered mouths) and gently invite quieter students to chime in. Use "group alerting" to keep everyone mentally present ("Everyone, listen to Maria and compare your ideas to hers"), and always allow for wait time after posing a question. If a conversation gets heated, shift the focus to the underlying idea, not the person who made a controversial or inappropriate comment, so learning continues. Finally, wrap it up with a chance to reflect, especially if emotions ran high. A simple writing prompt can help students process and cool down before moving on (Derek Bok Center for Teaching and Learning, 2024; Saphier et al., 2025; Vanderbilt University Center for Teaching, 2025).

Long-Term, High-Prep Strategies

Implement Partner Debate Instead of Partner Talk

In *Visible Learning: The Sequel*, Hattie (2023) emphasizes that teaching students to academically argue (with the text or one another)—rather than simply talk—is essential for deep learning. In addition, studies revealed that increased student talk, versus teacher talk, did not move the needle much in terms of increased student achievement (Groshell, 2024). What did increase academic outcomes related to the type of complex thinking students were engaging in through their discourse? Effective argumentation requires students to construct, defend, extend, and challenge ideas with evidence to foster critical thinking and reasoning. Although many classroom discussions encourage personal opinions, structured argumentation ensures students engage in disciplined, evidence-based discourse. Graff and Birkenstein (2024) similarly advocate for teaching students to engage in academic conversations by framing arguments within established written structures, whereas Biggs and colleagues (2022) underscore the importance of explicitly modeling and assessing argumentation skills. Moving from simple "turn and talk" to "turn and explicitly explain your thinking" in classroom discussions tends to produce an effect size of 0.82: a high influence per the Hattie (2024) model.

Teachers can follow a structured three-step approach to implement argumentation in K–12 classrooms quickly. This approach blends elements of the Oxford-Style House Debate from the UK (Versy, 2025), the Devil's Advocate Protocol from Australia (Bicksler, 2022), and the acknowledgment method.

- Assign students to opposing sides of a debatable issue—regardless of their personal beliefs—and require them to develop a structured case with evidence.
- Incorporate the Devil's Advocate Protocol by having students pause halfway through the debate and switch perspectives, forcing them to argue against their original position. This reversal approach deepens their ability to anticipate counterarguments and strengthens their reasoning skills—plus, it's pretty fun.
- Introduce an approach in which students respectfully acknowledge the validity of their opponent's strongest point before delivering their final rebuttal. This tactic fosters rhetorical discipline while reinforcing civil discourse, a skill essential for productive academic and nonacademic discussions.

When the teacher and content allow more time, students debate the question with research and literary analysis. For example, consider an English class analyzing dystopian literature that is presented with this prompt: Should governments be allowed to restrict individual freedoms for the greater good?

- Students are assigned to defend or oppose the idea, using evidence from *1984*, *Brave New World*, or real-world examples.
- After presenting their initial arguments, students must switch sides and argue the opposing viewpoint, strengthening their ability to anticipate counterarguments.
- Before students present their final arguments, they must first acknowledge at least one strong point from the other side. For example, they might say, "I can see how some government oversight helps prevent chaos, but history also proves that too much power can quickly turn oppressive." By practicing this skill, students get better at thinking critically, building stronger arguments, and analyzing ideas from multiple angles.

Teachers can introduce argument styles incorporating cultural storytelling and cooperative reasoning to extend the partner argument approach and challenge students further. The Ubuntu Dialogue method, popular in South Africa, works to get students planning together as a team to build arguments rather than individually competing against one another (Marovah & Mutanga, 2023). The focus is on collaboration and the sharing of ideas, not just winning debates. Teachers can also try other strategies, such as having students use imagery instead of direct statements, a shift that encourages more creativity. For example, students might present their argument in the form of a myth, fable, or historical anecdote before revealing the logical reasoning behind their position. These methods enhance argumentation skills and encourage a more sophisticated (and culturally rich) understanding of persuasion, logic, and discourse.

In one 6th grade social studies class in Wisconsin, students were studying folktales in English class. Instead of directly debating whether protecting the environment is important, students crafted short folktales for arguments. On the day Keith observed, one group told a story of a village that neglected their river, causing it to dry up, and another told of villagers who cared for their river, creating prosperity. After sharing their stories, students then discussed the real-world reasons behind their positions. This approach sparked creativity, deepened their understanding of persuasive techniques, and helped them think critically about real-life issues.

Create Differentiated Tasks

When teachers offer activity choices that cater to students' unique interests, they allow students to show what they have learned in multiple ways. Students can be given choices that speak to their talents and interests but still demonstrate mastery of the standard. A couple of examples illustrate this.

An ELA class studied poetry for a couple of weeks. They read and analyzed several poems with the teacher's help. The teacher did a powerful job of guided practice with the students, moving them to very high-level thinking, but wanted to see what the students could do on their own. The students selected a poem by an author they studied and showed their understanding of the author's meaning and intention in one of four ways: (1) write a literary analysis; (2) draw or paint their interpretation and write an explanation of that artistic interpretation; (3) adapt the poem to an original musical score and explain why the music depicted the author's intent; or (4) rewrite the poem as an original short story that clarifies the author's intent. The teacher also left the activity open to other approved ideas. The students enjoyed the assignment, and the results demonstrated unique comprehension from each student.

By contrast, in a 3rd grade class, a teacher had been teaching multiplication and division. Students could follow directions and do the algorithms, but the teacher wanted to see whether they understood the relationship between the mathematical ideas and the underlying concepts. The students came into class one day, and on two big tables were all kinds of things: candy bars, pencils, jacks, erasers, sets of pictures, cards, and so on. Students were put in pairs, and the only directions were to "use something from the table to tell a story that includes division and multiplication." The stories were highly diverse, but as students listened to one another, they solidified their understanding of the mathematical concepts.

Although offering differentiated tasks by providing choices based on students' interests or preferred styles of learning has shown a modest direct impact on standardized academic achievement, there are reasons to use this strategy occasionally in the classroom: Differentiated tasks may boost student engagement, promote autonomy, honor diverse strengths, and help students develop valuable life skills beyond academics. The indirect benefits of differentiation—such as enhanced engagement, deeper learning, inclusivity, and development of critical life skills—justify judiciously and occasionally employing this approach as part of a balanced instructional repertoire.

Use Interactive Writing Strategies

Engaging students in writing need not be a solitary, silent activity. In fact, writing can become one of the most vibrant, collaborative parts of the school day. When students interact around writing, they build their skills while sharing creativity, reflecting on experiences, and deepening their understanding of content. The following interactive writing strategies transform writing from a chore into an adventure, encouraging learners to explore language, stories, poetry, and more—together. These strategies are collected from years of working with outstanding writing teachers and some of our favorite authors on writing: Graff and Birkenstein (2024) and Roth and Dabrowski (2023).

- **Collaborative Story Weaving:** Students collectively craft a narrative, with each contributing sentences or paragraphs. This process promotes teamwork and sparks creativity as the story evolves in unexpected directions.
- **Interactive Sentence Construction:** Learners build sentences together, intentionally focusing on grammar, syntax, and sentence combining. By literally constructing sentences side by side—perhaps on a whiteboard or by arranging word and phrase cutouts—students can see how language fits together in real time. This collaborative, hands-on process strengthens their understanding of sentence formation and reinforces key writing conventions.
- **Shared Journal Entries:** A communal journal, maintained by the class (perhaps even electronically), allows students to take turns contributing entries on rotating topics. This is a reflective, low-pressure way to encourage regular writing.

- **Group Research Summaries:** Students collaboratively research a topic, combining their findings into cohesive summaries. Done on a shared digital document, each student's contribution can be color-coded to ensure individual and group accountability. This activity integrates research skills and collaborative writing practice.

- **Peer Review Workshops:** Learners exchange writing drafts and provide thoughtful feedback to peers, sharpening their critical thinking and editing skills and promoting mutual growth.

- **Class Anthology Projects:** Students submit individual writing pieces into a collective anthology. They experience the publishing process firsthand, developing pride and ownership in their writing.

- **Interactive Digital Storytelling:** Students collaboratively create digital stories using multimedia tools, merging traditional storytelling with technology, which boosts engagement and tech literacy.

- **Role-Play Dialogues:** Students write and perform dialogues based on curricular themes, deepening their understanding through drama and active participation. In one social studies lesson on the American Revolution, students paired up and wrote a dialogue between George Washington and King George III. They collaboratively researched their perspectives, drafted authentic-sounding conversations, and then performed their dialogues for the class, enhancing their grasp of historical viewpoints through drama. In a science class, students studying ecosystems formed small groups and scripted a dialogue-based debate among different organisms (e.g., a predator, its prey, and a plant). Each student embodied their chosen role, advocating for their character's importance within the ecosystem. Performing the dialogues reinforced their understanding of ecological interdependence through active participation and dramatization.

- **Themed Poetry Circles:** Learners compose poems on assigned themes and then share them in supportive group settings, fostering creative poetic expression and group discussion.

- **Collective Editing Sessions:** An entire class works in small groups or as a whole group to edit a piece of writing. Students learn revision and proofreading techniques by seeing these skills modeled and practiced collectively.

- **Interactive Writing:** The teacher and students jointly compose text, with the teacher actively modeling, scaffolding, and guiding every step of the writing process with the student.

- **Guided Writing:** Students are in small, skill-based groups where they write more independently, applying previously taught strategies while the teacher circulates to provide targeted feedback and support as needed. Interactive writing (above) is teacher-led and collaborative, whereas guided writing is student-driven with light, responsive teacher coaching.

- **Language Experience Approach:** Students orally narrate personal experiences, which the teacher transcribes or helps students record using speech-to-text software. These transcriptions become personalized reading material, directly linking students' spoken language to written literacy. A savvy teacher could even load the story into generative AI software and adjust the story to the appropriate comprehension level needed by the student.

- **Process Writing:** Traditionally, process writing emphasizes several key steps—planning, drafting, revising, and editing—and has a strong research-backed track record (effect size = .50; Hattie, 2024). Though commonly used for individual student work, this multistage approach naturally lends itself to collaboration. Students can plan writing projects together, draft texts alongside peers, revise their work through peer feedback sessions, and even edit collaboratively with classmates, teachers, or family members. By making each step collaborative, students gain a deeper appreciation for writing as a shared craft rather than a solitary task.

- **Writing Workshops:** Typically, a writing workshop consists of three main components: a minilesson, independent writing time, and share time. During the minilesson, the teacher explicitly instructs a specific writing skill or strategy, often modeling it for the class. Following this work, students write independently, applying the lesson's focus to their work. The session concludes with share time, when selected students present their writing to the class, fostering a sense of community and shared learning. To enhance the collaborative aspects of a writing workshop, educators can incorporate peer interactions throughout the process. For example, during independent writing, students can pair up to discuss their ideas, offer feedback, and assist each other in revising and editing their work. This encourages students to critically engage with each other's writing, which promotes a deeper understanding of the writing process. Additionally, group brainstorming activities can be introduced during the planning stages; this allows students to collectively generate ideas and support one another in developing their narratives. By integrating these collaborative elements, writing workshops develop individual writing stamina and cultivate a supportive community of writers who learn from and inspire one another.

- **Writing Conferences:** Regular small-group meetings between the teacher and small cohorts of students occur to discuss writing progress, set goals, and address targeted challenges, ensuring personalized support in a small, collaborative setting.

- **Interactive Writing Notebooks:** Personalized notebooks serve as spaces where students engage in various writing activities, reflect on their learning, and track their writing growth over time.

This chapter offers a toolkit of practical, research-based ways to keep students actively engaged in learning at every grade level. It moves from quick, low-prep ideas—such as energizing warm-ups, clear lesson goals, whisper feedback, and whole-class participation techniques—to moderate-prep strategies, such as peer coaching, accountable reading, and flexible grouping that promote collaboration and reflection. The chapter concludes with high-prep approaches, including structured debates, differentiated projects, and interactive writing, which collectively challenge students to think critically, communicate creatively, and connect their learning to real-world contexts. Together, these strategies help teachers build classrooms that are lively, inclusive, and driven by genuine student curiosity and ownership.

2

Classroom Management: Affective Learning Gaps

Routine, Moderate-Prep Strategies

Long-Term, High-Prep Strategies

Teachers today often share that managing classrooms feels more demanding than ever. Although behavior and emotional challenges have always been part of teaching, many educators sense these issues are popping up more often and becoming harder to handle. Students now come to school with heavier emotional burdens and trickier behaviors, making it even more challenging to maintain a calm and productive classroom atmosphere. Nevertheless, there's some good news: There are plenty of proven, practical strategies out there—tested by real teachers and backed by solid research—that can help establish a calm, supportive classroom environment, and we've gathered the best of the best.

This chapter is packed with more than 60 straightforward, innovative ideas teachers can use immediately, no matter what grade level they teach. These strategies will help students manage their behaviors better, build emotional strength, and create an atmosphere of trust and active engagement. Many of the ideas presented here are drawn from *Confident Classroom Management Moves* (Young, 2025).

This chapter's strategies are grouped into three categories reflecting how much time and preparation each takes:

- Immediate, Low-Prep Strategies
- Routine, Moderate-Prep Strategies
- Long-Term, High-Prep Strategies

Now let's jump in and make classrooms calmer, happier, and more productive for both teachers and students.

Immediate, Low-Prep Strategies

Forecast Growth to Shape Behavior

Students often live up—or down—to the expectations set for them. Hattie (2023) found that teacher expectations carry an average effect size of 0.58 on student achievement, making them one of the most powerful influences in education. When teachers consistently point out even minor improvements in behavior, students begin to internalize these messages and see themselves as capable of growth. For example, if a student who usually disrupts class enters quietly one morning, the teacher might note, "I saw how you came in calmly and got right to work—that shows focus." Such language affirms desired traits and speaks positive identities into reality (Young, 2025). Over time, students begin to perceive themselves as responsible and capable of positive change, strengthening both self-belief and classroom climate (Bilmes, 2012; Saphier et al., 2025). It's a bit like watching a Polaroid develop in your hand; positive forecasted expectations act as the developer fluid, and the image of "who I can be" appears because you aimed the camera there.

Engage in Thoughtful Acts of Care

Purposefully showing kindness helps students feel that they truly belong in class (Noddings, 2013). Simple gestures—such as greeting students by name, remembering what they care about, and recognizing small achievements—build trust and foster a positive learning climate. For instance, Young and colleagues (2023) describe how effective teachers intentionally use caring routines such as greeting students individually, using preferred names, and showing personal interest to establish safety and emotional connection. Similarly, Bilmes (2012) notes that when teachers focus on children's strengths and offer genuine acknowledgment rather than reprimand, students begin to see themselves as valued members of the community.

For example, one teacher noticed a student loved soccer, so she started casually asking how his games went. Gradually, this small habit turned their previously strained relationship into friendly, everyday chats. Keith and Angela observed that the teacher kindly greeted tardy students in one classroom. "Good morning. Your materials are on your desks; we'll catch you up as we go." When asked, the teacher explained that the two students walked a half-mile and then rode two buses to get to school. She admitted that when they first started arriving late, she scolded them and threatened them with detentions for their tardiness. Over time, she got to know them and heard their stories. Then she realized they made significant efforts to get to school and that it would be easy for them to give up. From then on, she simply ensured that all materials were on their desks and often left a little note with something like "I know you have had a busy morning. Take a breath!" This simple act of teacher kindness resulted in two students working very hard and keeping up with the class.

Give Acknowledgment Beyond the Classroom

Recognition outside the classroom reinforces students' sense of worth. Simple acknowledgments in spaces such as hallways or lunchrooms can have a lasting impact. In the hallway: "I saw you helping your friend carry books—kindness like that makes our school a better place!" In the lunchroom: "I noticed you stayed on task in class today, even when others were distracted. That kind of focus will take you far!" These brief, genuine interactions help students see that the teacher's care extends beyond academic settings, building trust and rapport that strengthen classroom relationships (Young, 2025). These acknowledgments function like small push notifications—quick alerts that remind students their effort matters no matter where they are on campus.

Use Humor and Creativity to Redirect Behavior

A touch of genuine, lighthearted humor can reset attention, ease tension, and prevent power struggles when used with warmth and care. Humor works best when it builds connection rather than control, and it should invite students back into learning—not make them the punchline. It's similar to releasing a bit of air from a balloon instead of popping it; humor vents tension without causing embarrassment or disruption. Avoid sarcasm or humor at a student's expense, as those forms erode trust and belonging. Instead, use humor that highlights shared humanity, imagination, or gentle exaggeration.

With this in mind, teachers might

- **Channel excess energy playfully:** When a preschooler wiggles during circle time, say, "Looks like your wiggles are ready to dance! Let's save them for recess and see your best moves then."
- **Recast transitions as a game:** If the line is forming slowly, try, "Our invisible line leader must still be getting ready—let's show them how it's done!"
- **Reframe chatter as curiosity:** When small groups grow noisy, say, "Sounds like our brains are thinking out loud—let's whisper-think for a bit so everyone's ideas can fit in the room."
- **Normalize challenge through humor:** When a student sighs over a tough problem, smile and respond, "That's your brain getting stronger—it grumbles a little when it grows!"
- **Redirect repetitive tapping or fidgeting:** Laugh gently and say, "We might have the next great drummer here! Let's rest those drumsticks so you're ready for the concert later."

- **Reenergize a tired class:** After lunch, suggest, "If our brains had batteries, we'd be on 10 percent. Let's recharge—stand up, stretch, and give me your best superhero pose!"
- **Calm premature packing:** When students start rustling before the bell, grin and say, "Ah, the sound of zippers—the universal signal of rebellion! Let's hold that revolution until I finish this one last point."
- **Ease quiz anxiety:** Before a test, lighten the mood and say, "Relax—it's not a pop quiz; it's a surprise opportunity to shine!"
- **Reframe restlessness with empathy:** When a student can't sit still, whisper, "Looks like your energy wants to learn, too—let's help it join us quietly."

These quick, creative comments acknowledge behavior without confrontation, reduce anxiety and boredom—both known detractors from achievement (Hattie, 2023)—and strengthen rapport. As Young (2025) emphasizes, humor used kindly and sparingly "redirects, not reprimands," keeping the classroom calm, safe, and human. Used thoughtfully, it reminds students that learning is serious work, but classrooms can still be joyful places.

Encourage Self-Reflection and Problem Solving

Helping students notice when they're feeling frustrated can stop emotions from bubbling over. For example, a teacher might ask, "Is this a big deal, a medium deal, or just a little thing?"—a prompt that allows students to assess the size of their reaction and calm down before emotions escalate. This practice draws on two high-impact influences identified in Visible Learning research—self-judgment and reflection (effect size = 0.81) and metacognitive strategies (effect size = 0.58)—both strongly associated with student achievement (Hattie, 2023).

In one kindergarten classroom, the teacher—nicknamed "the kindergartener whisperer" by her colleagues—used a kinesthetic reflection routine to help children self-regulate. When a student's behavior drifted off track, she asked them to whisper what they were doing—such as *talking loudly* or *squirming*—into their "bubble," made by cupping their hands in front of their mouths. Then the students closed their eyes, thought quietly about how that behavior compared with what they *should* be doing, and gently adjusted their actions. This brief self-reflection helped students recognize their choices and practice independent problem solving. Such strategies mirror the coaching approaches described by Young and colleagues (2023), who note that inviting students to self-reflect builds calm, ownership, and social-emotional growth. Likewise, Bilmes (2012) demonstrates that guiding young learners to pause and notice their emotions strengthens self-regulation and reduces disruptive behavior.

Eliminate Sarcasm to Foster a Safe Environment

Although some teachers use sarcasm to connect with students or lighten the mood, over a century of research shows that it consistently undermines emotional safety in classrooms. As early as the 1920s, studies by Laird (1923) and Briggs (1928) documented the negative effects of sarcastic teacher remarks on student motivation and trust. Nearly a hundred years later, Saphier and colleagues (2025) confirmed that sarcasm remains one of the most destructive yet persistent habits in teaching, eroding relationships and creating climates of fear rather than belonging. A comment like, "Oh great, another forgotten assignment—you're on a roll!" may be intended as humor, but it can discourage a struggling student or confuse one who processes language literally. For students with anxiety, learning differences, or trauma histories, sarcastic remarks can feel like ridicule rather than rapport. Even students who are not the direct target—such as the quiet child in the back who worries they might be next—absorb the tension such remarks create. Students listen with their hearts as much as their ears; when sarcasm lands, even unintended bystanders feel unsafe. Sarcasm functions like screen glare: harsh, fatiguing, and harmful to those who are most sensitive. A teacher's tone benefits from a figurative blue-light filter that softens communication and protects emotional safety.

Replacing sarcasm with clear, respectful language builds trust and predictability. Instead of saying, "Nice of you to join us," when a student arrives late, a teacher might calmly say, "I'm glad you're here—grab your materials, and let's get started." This kind of communication signals care and stability rather than judgment. Eliminating sarcasm is not about losing humor—it's about ensuring every student, including those who are most vulnerable, feels emotionally safe in the room. When teachers choose clarity and kindness over cutting humor, they model the professional respect that sustains authentic connection and collective trust (Young, 2025).

Repair and Maintain Connections After Corrections

Discipline should never come at the expense of the student-teacher relationship. Research confirms that strong relationships are among the most powerful influences on learning, with an average effect size of 0.57 (Hattie, 2023). A student who feels personally rejected is far less likely to respond positively to redirection, so effective teachers focus on the behavior—not the person—when correcting. A calm, neutral message, such as "Hey, we're fine; I just need you to change what you're doing," communicates respect and maintains connection. This wording clearly separates the behavior from the individual, showing the concern is about the action, not the student's worth.

Following up later also reinforces care and trust. For example, if a student struggles early in the day, the teacher might later quietly say, "I noticed you had a rough start this morning, but I was proud of how you pulled it together." That brief acknowledgment repairs any tension and reminds the student that the relationship is intact. Young and colleagues (2023) describe this as *relationship repair*—the deliberate act of checking back in with students after a conflict to model empathy and rebuild emotional safety. Similarly, Bilmes (2012) shows that when teachers address misbehavior calmly and reconnect afterward, children learn that guidance is supportive rather than punitive. When students feel that their teacher genuinely cares and respects them—even during correction—they are less likely to resist and more likely to re-engage in learning.

Foster a Culture of Appreciation

Recognizing positive behaviors fosters teamwork, kindness, and a sense of belonging. Appreciation is more than praise—it's about noticing effort, naming contribution, and nurturing genuine connection. Teachers can weave acknowledgment into daily routines through "kindness jars," peer shout-outs, and class helpers who check on absent students or share notes of encouragement. These small rituals transform appreciation from a one-time gesture into a community norm that reinforces empathy and shared responsibility (Bailey, 2021; Bilmes, 2012; Sprick et al., 2021; Young et al., 2023).

Appreciation also means valuing each student's voice. As Noddings (2013) explains, caring is an ethical practice of "seeing" others with respect, while Lemov and colleagues (2022) highlight that daily dignity practices build belonging and shared purpose. Teachers might say, "Show your appreciation with eyes and ears on the speaker," or "Please jot that idea in your notes and credit it to Juan." Such routines promote respectful dialogue and equitable participation—key ingredients of effective classroom climate and student engagement (Hattie, 2023; Saphier et al., 2025). When appreciation becomes part of the classroom culture, students experience gratitude not just from the teacher but from one another, creating a community that is connected, responsible, and caring.

Use Positive Framing to Guide Behavior

Changing how directions are phrased can shift students' attention toward positive actions instead of prohibitions. When teachers state what they want to see—rather than what to stop—they create clarity and preserve momentum (Bailey, 2021; Saphier et al., 2025; Sprick et al., 2021). For instance, instead of saying, "Stop talking," an elementary teacher might say, "Let's all jump into question one together," or "Show me listening bodies for our read-aloud." This keeps students focused on the desired behavior and signals that the teacher expects cooperation rather than compliance through correction (Bilmes, 2012; Hattie, 2023).

In middle and high school settings, positive framing works just as effectively. A teacher might replace "No phones out!" with "Let's keep our focus on the lab data for the next five minutes," or shift "Don't run!" to "Walk with purpose to your next class." Sprick (2021) and PBIS (2022) emphasize that consistently phrasing expectations as actions ("Do this...") rather than restrictions ("Don't...") reinforces routines, reduces resistance, and helps students internalize pro-social norms. Over time, students learn to anticipate what productive behavior looks like, improving both classroom climate and self-regulation (Bailey, 2021; Hattie, 2023; Sprick, 2021). Whether with 5-year-olds or 15-year-olds, positive framing is about teaching expectations as clearly as content. It models respectful communication, maintains pacing, and turns management moments into opportunities for belonging and growth.

Actively Monitor and Engage

Students are less likely to misbehave when they feel noticed and valued. Circulating around the room, giving immediate feedback, and acknowledging effort keep students engaged. This kind of movement mirrors a Wi-Fi walk test: moving through the space to identify where engagement is strong, fading, or disconnected. For example, a teacher walking around and highlighting correct answers during math encourages others to stay focused. A school in Illinois calls this method "Wonder, Don't Wander," meaning that as teachers move around the room, they are intentional about seeing who is learning and who is not. For example, suppose a student struggles to begin or continue working during an independent work assignment. The teacher can take a moment and develop a question or a specific, actionable piece of feedback to help move the student forward. For example, "When I am trying to get thoughts out of my head onto paper, sometimes it helps just to brainstorm some words. Take 20 seconds and write at least five words you know about this assignment."

Reinforce Positive Behavior and Effort

Acknowledging effort—rather than merely praising outcomes—helps students internalize motivation and view success as the result of persistence. Instead of saying, "Good job!" teachers can use acknowledgment language such as "I noticed you stuck with that problem even when it got tricky," or "I saw how carefully you explained your idea." These specific, effort-focused statements strengthen self-regulation and reinforce desired behaviors without fostering dependence on praise (Bailey, 2021; Bilmes, 2012; Saphier et al., 2025; Sprick, 2021). Sprick and colleagues (2021) and PBIS (2022) both identify this approach as a support that builds engagement and accountability for all students. Hattie (2023) highlights explicit feedback as one of the most influential factors in learning (effect size = 0.70), while Hammond (2025) and Lemov and colleagues (2022) note that acknowledgment of effort builds students' "learning power" and sense of belonging. Noddings (2013) adds that noticing and naming effort is an ethical act of care—it tells students their work and persistence are seen and valued.

At every grade level, effort-based acknowledgment looks slightly different but carries the same message of respect:

- **Preschool:** "You kept trying to zip your coat even when it was tricky. That's called persistence."
- **Elementary:** "I noticed you reread that paragraph to check your understanding—great focus! How can you remind yourself to do that moving forward?"
- **Middle school:** "You stayed calm when your group disagreed and helped everyone get back on track. How did that make you feel?"
- **High school:** "You revised your lab report and addressed my feedback—that kind of effort builds real skill."

Effort-focused acknowledgment shifts classroom culture from compliance to growth. When teachers intentionally name what students *did*—not just that they "did well"—they teach perseverance, reflection, and pride in progress.

Use a Dramatic Pause

Sometimes the most powerful classroom management move is to say nothing at all. If students drift off task, the teacher can stop mid-sentence, sip water, or simply let the silence stretch. The stillness itself signals expectation and composure—students often self-correct as one quietly whispers, "Oh, we should stop." Used consistently, this technique builds anticipation and draws attention back to the speaker, much like a skilled storyteller commanding an audience (Bailey, 2021; Bilmes, 2012; Saphier et al., 2025; Young, 2025). Sprick (2021) and Sprick and colleagues (2021) note that brief, silent pauses act as universal practices that reset focus without confrontation. Hammond (2025) adds that calm, deliberate silence models emotional regulation, while Lemov and colleagues (2022) and Noddings

(2013) describe such restraint as a mark of respect and relational care.

In a kindergarten classroom, a teacher might simply stop reading and place a finger on the page until the group settles. In high school, a teacher might cap a marker, take a slow sip of water, and wait. The silence itself communicates confidence and composure; it says, "I trust you to notice what needs to happen next." Research shows that teachers' calmness and classroom climate directly enhance engagement and learning (Center on Positive Behavioral Interventions and Supports, 2022; Hattie, 2023). Strategic silence turns self-regulation into a shared classroom norm.

Let the Student Have the Last Word

This move is one of the hardest for teachers to master—but also one of the most powerful. When a student mutters a defiant comment like "This is dumb," the teacher's best response is often calm neutrality. Instead of reacting, debating, or defending the lesson, the teacher can quietly say, "Noted," or simply move on. This pause communicates confidence and self-control, modeling the composure that students need to learn (Saphier et al., 2025; Sprick, 2021). Sprick and colleagues (2021) and PBIS (2022) identify this form of temporary nonengagement as a response that frequently stops escalation and preserves classroom climate. Lemov and colleagues (2022) and Noddings (2013) note that such restraint protects student dignity while maintaining the teacher's authority.

However, letting a student have the last word does not mean ignoring misbehavior indefinitely. Once emotions cool and the class has moved forward, the teacher can address the issue privately and directly. That later conversation—away from peers— reestablishes boundaries without public embarrassment. As Bailey (2021) explains, connection and correction work best in sequence: first calm, then coach. In practice, an elementary teacher might acknowledge a frustrated comment with a quiet nod and return to instruction, checking in with the student during recess. A secondary teacher might respond to a sarcastic remark with a brief, neutral "We'll talk after class" and continue teaching. The restraint in the moment is deliberate, not passive—it communicates professionalism, trust, and control. Over time, this disciplined calm builds a classroom culture where authority rests on respect, not volume.

Gesture Instead of Speak

Quiet gestures can often redirect students more effectively than words. These gestures function like subtitles: silent but fully communicative, conveying meaning without disrupting the main audio of the lesson. Eye contact, a subtle head shake, or a tap on the wrist to indicate time can communicate expectations without interrupting instruction. Nonverbal cues preserve the flow of the lesson and allow students to self-correct while maintaining dignity (Bailey, 2021; Bilmes, 2012; Saphier et al., 2025; Sprick et al., 2021; Young, 2025). Teachers can also be transparent about their approach. A private explanation, such as "I look at you so you can choose whether others know you're off task. I don't want to call you out verbally," lets students understand that nonverbal signals are about respect, not control. Sprick (2021) and PBIS (2022) identify this tactic as a universal move for all students, which potentially prevents escalation and strengthens positive classroom habits.

In preschool or elementary settings, teachers might use a simple raised finger for "eyes on me," a gentle tap on a desk, or a quiet proximity cue to guide behavior. In a secondary school, a teacher might pause briefly, make calm eye contact, or tilt their head toward a task sheet to prompt reengagement. These small actions carry weight because they model composure and confidence. Hattie (2023) and Hammond (2025) note that such nonverbal regulation supports learning by lowering anxiety and maintaining psychological safety, while Lemov and colleagues (2022) and Noddings (2013) remind us that subtlety communicates care and professionalism.

Move Closer to Redirect Behavior

Physical proximity is one of the simplest and most effective ways to redirect off-task behavior. The effect resembles stepping back into Bluetooth range; once you're near, the connection resets without any verbal command. When a student starts whispering or drifting from the task, the teacher can casually walk closer, maintain neutral body language, and quietly say, "We're focusing right now." This subtle move reminds students of expectations without embarrassment or confrontation (Bailey, 2021; Bilmes, 2012; Saphier et al., 2025; Sprick et al., 2021).

Sprick (2021) and PBIS (2022) identify proximity as a proactive universal strategy for all students that promotes attention and reduces disruptions without interrupting instruction. Hattie (2023) and Hammond (2025) explain that calm, relational teacher presence enhances classroom climate and student regulation. Lemov and colleagues (2022) and Noddings (2013) add that proximity communicates care and attentiveness; it's about connection, not control. In middle or high school, a teacher might pause near a pair of chatting students and rest a hand on a nearby desk, allowing silence and presence to do the work. Small shifts like these can redirect behavior before it grows, signaling authority and trust without confrontation.

Highlight Behavior Without Names

Instead of focusing attention on misbehavior, teachers can build engagement by noticing and naming positive actions. A simple comment such as "I see three people already getting started—love it" shifts the tone from correction to encouragement. Using a collective cue like "I see 98 percent of students ready to read; I need 100 percent" leverages positive reinforcement and peer influence to guide the last few students to follow without embarrassment (Bailey, 2021; Lemov et al., 2022; Sprick et al., 2021). It operates like adjusting channels on a mixing board: amplifying the desired behaviors so the whole room tunes to the same frequency. Saphier and colleagues (2025) explain that this redirection works because it reinforces norms rather than highlighting errors, while Sprick (2021) and PBIS (2022) describe it as a proactive technique for use with all students and one that builds compliance through consistent, calm, and neutral acknowledgment. Bilmes (2012) and Noddings (2013) further remind educators that recognition rooted in care and belonging is more sustainable than superficial praise.

In early childhood classrooms, this "highlighting behavior you want to see" might sound like, "I see friends sitting on their 'sit spot' [floor dot, sit upon, carpet marker, etc.] and ready for the story—beautiful listening!" In a secondary school, it could be "I see one group already comparing notes; let's all get to that point." These statements set clear expectations while maintaining dignity and trust. Positive framing and visible reinforcement strengthen classroom culture and improve attention, with research showing classroom climate as a strong predictor of academic success (Hattie, 2023; PBIS, 2022; Saphier et al., 2025).

Redirect and Move On

Sometimes the most powerful classroom management move is the least intrusive one. Redirecting and moving on gives students a chance to self-correct without public pressure or emotional confrontation. By calmly placing work in front of a distracted student and saying, "You need to complete this, and I know you'll make the right choice," the teacher signals confidence in the student's ability to recover and refocus. The key lies in brevity and trust—delivering the cue, then walking away (Bailey, 2021; Bilmes, 2012; Saphier et al., 2025; Young, 2025). This approach models self-control and communicates that the teacher doesn't need to win a power struggle. As Sprick (2021) notes, quiet direction followed by distance helps prevent escalation and preserve dignity. Sprick and colleagues (2021) and PBIS (2022) categorize these "low-intensity redirections" as simple, proactive interventions that keep instruction flowing for all students. Noddings (2013) and Lemov and colleagues (2022) add that this restraint conveys ethical care and trust, demonstrating to students that they are capable of making better choices without overcorrection.

What does this look like in action? In a preschool or elementary setting, a teacher might slide a crayon box toward a child who's stalling during art and say softly, "You know what to do," before walking away. In middle or high school, a teacher might calmly place work in front of a student who is checking their phone, and whisper, "Let's get back to it," and then resume teaching. The act itself—brief, confident, and devoid of emotional charge—is both brave and strategic. Hattie (2023) and Hammond (2025) affirm that classrooms where teachers project calm trust foster higher self-regulation and engagement. Redirecting and moving on takes courage—it's the teacher's quiet way of saying, "I believe you'll handle this right."

Correct Privately When Possible

Public corrections often cause embarrassment, resistance, or disconnection. Instead of calling out a misbehavior in front of the class, the teacher quietly approaches the student and says, "Let's talk about this after class," or offers a brief, neutral cue to redirect attention. This private approach helps maintain student cooperation and trust while still addressing the behavior (Bailey, 2021; Bilmes, 2012; Sprick, 2021). In a preschool or elementary classroom, this might mean moving across the room and kneeling beside a child to whisper, "Let's talk about what's happening," rather than yelling the student's name across the room. In middle or high school, a teacher might calmly pass by a student's desk and say quietly, "Let's talk right after the bell." The goal is to correct without publicly identifying or embarrassing the student. It's essentially the classroom equivalent of sending a private direct message instead of posting publicly. It's quiet correction without the audience.

Research confirms that relational climate and teacher–student connection are among the strongest predictors of student engagement and achievement (Hattie, 2023; Saphier et al., 2025). Similarly, Lemov and colleagues (2022) describe dignity-preserving corrections as "relationship deposits," and Noddings (2013) defines such discretion as a moral act of care. When feedback is private, calm, and consistent, it strengthens trust and often reduces escalation.

Support Reentry into the Group

After a misbehavior, students need reassurance that they still belong while being held accountable for their choices. A brief, positive statement such as "Glad you're back—let's keep up the positive choices" communicates both forgiveness and expectation. Reentry works like pressing "resume" on a paused program: continuing where learning left off without wiping the slate clean unnecessarily. This moment of reconnection—what Bailey (2021) calls "connection before correction"—helps students return to learning without shame while maintaining classroom order (Bilmes, 2012; Hattie, 2023; Noddings, 2013). Across grade levels, the reentry can take many forms. In a preschool or elementary classroom, a teacher might welcome a child back to the carpet circle with a smile and a nod, then cue a peer to make space beside them. In middle or high school, a teacher might quietly check in at the student's desk and say, "Good to have you back; let's jump in where we left off." These gestures show that discipline is corrective rather than punitive and that the relationship remains intact (Lemov et al., 2022; Saphier et al., 2025; Sprick, 2021).

PBIS (2022) and Sprick and colleagues (2021) identify these brief but intentional reentry interactions as Tier 1 and Tier 2 supports—Tier 1 for universal practices for all students that maintain community, and Tier 2 for students needing extra support when patterns of behavior recur. Restoring a sense of belonging after discipline enhances motivation, reinforces responsibility, and fosters a classroom climate in which students trust that mistakes can lead to growth.

Use an Emotional Temperature Check

Before addressing a conflict or off-task behavior, teachers can ask students to rate their level of frustration on a scale from 1 to 10. If the number is high—usually above a 7—it signals the need for calm before problem solving. A brief pause for breathing, grounding, or quiet time helps students regulate and return to a thinking state (Bailey, 2021; Bilmes, 2012; Honsinger & Brown, 2019; PBIS, 2022). For example, an elementary teacher might say, "On a scale from 1 to 10, how big does this feel right now?" and then guide the student in slow breaths before continuing the conversation. In a high school setting, a teacher might ask privately, "How intense is this for you on a 1–10 scale?" and offer a few minutes to cool off before revisiting the issue. These check-ins help students pause, label their emotions, and recognize that feelings fluctuate—skills that contribute to emotional maturity and self-control.

Research supports this approach: self-regulation and the emotional climate have among the highest influences on student success (Hattie, 2023; Hammond, 2025). Saphier and colleagues (2025) note that emotionally savvy teachers can deescalate conflicts before they spread, while Sprick and colleagues (2021) remind educators that calm monitoring and consistent follow-through sustain safety and trust. Using temperature checks as routine supports teaches students that emotions can be acknowledged and managed without judgment—an act of both empathy and professionalism.

Encourage Grounding with 5-4-3-2-1

Grounding techniques help students refocus when emotions or stress take over. The 5-4-3-2-1 strategy invites students to name five things they see, four things they can touch, three things they hear, two things they smell, and one thing they taste. This brief sensory exercise helps anchor attention in the present moment and slows the body's stress response (Bailey, 2021; Bilmes, 2012; Honsinger & Brown, 2019; PBIS, 2022; Young, 2025). In early childhood and elementary settings, a teacher might guide the class through the steps aloud—"Look for five colors you can name"—to redirect collective classroom energy after transitions. In middle or high school, a teacher could quietly walk a distressed student through the process, adding optional sensory resets such as taking a sip of water or squeezing a stress ball. Each sense-based focus helps the student reconnect with their environment and regain control.

Research underscores that practices supporting self-regulation produce significant gains in learning and emotional balance. Hattie (2023) reports an effect size of approximately 0.75 for self-regulation, while Hammond (2025) describes how attention to sensory and emotional balance builds the "attentional architecture" needed for learning. Saphier and others (2025) further emphasize that such calm, structured routines create predictable environments where students feel safe to recover. Grounding not only diffuses immediate stress but also teaches students how to restore calm independently —a caring act that builds trust and belonging.

Use a Neutral, Nonconfrontational Tone

Escalating conflicts rarely leads to positive outcomes. A neutral tone acts like noise-canceling technology: quieting the emotional static so students can concentrate on the actual message. When teachers respond with calm neutrality instead of emotion, they model composure and preserve student dignity. A measured tone—steady, even, and slightly indifferent—prevents power struggles and signals confidence (Bailey, 2021; Bilmes, 2012; Saphier et al., 2025; Young, 2025). When a student yells in frustration, the teacher might take a breath, keep their voice quiet, and reply with mild indifference, such as "Yes, and try again." This kind of tone is neither angry nor sarcastic; it is *boring on purpose*. Sometimes the best deescalation is sounding uninterested in the drama. Teachers might vary their neutral tone depending on the moment:

- A flat or bored tone conveys "This isn't exciting for me; let's move on."
- A mildly curious tone, such as "Hmm, that didn't work. What's next?" signals reflection, not judgment.
- A softly amused tone, along with a faint smile and "Well, that's one way to do it," reframes tension without mockery.

In early elementary grades, this might sound like a teacher calmly repeating, "We use kind words—try again," with a relaxed face and an even tone. In middle or high school, a teacher might lower their voice slightly and say, "You're upset, I hear that. Take a second—then let's figure this out." The tone communicates authority without aggression and keeps the exchange safe.

Sprick (2021) and PBIS (2022) identify neutral verbal delivery as one of the most effective tactics for preventing escalation, while Hammond (2025) and Hattie (2023) link teacher composure to improved classroom climate and student focus. Noddings (2013) and Lemov and colleagues (2022) add that a calm, steady tone models care and emotional balance, teaching students that conflict can be met with control rather than confrontation. Neutrality doesn't mean detachment; it means emotional discipline in service of trust. Over time, consistent calm responses teach students to mirror the same steadiness in themselves.

Lower Speech Volume and Speed

A calm teacher leads to a calm classroom. Before responding to off-task or emotional behavior, lowering one's voice and slowing speech can deescalate tension and invite reflection. A teacher might take a slow breath and softly say, "I'm going to speak quietly so we can think this through together." This small change shifts the tone from reactive to reflective, signaling safety and control (Bailey, 2021; Bilmes, 2012; Saphier et al., 2025). Sometimes speaking in a hushed, almost secretive tone—"I have something important to tell you, but only if you're ready to listen"—can spark curiosity and draw students in (Young, 2025). Whispering calmly, rather than raising the voice, models emotional self-regulation and restores focus. As Sprick (2021) and PBIS (2022) note, measured communication is one of the most effective prevention tools for classroom conflict.

In younger grades, this may mean lowering the voice and moving physically closer to a child while maintaining eye contact; for secondary students, a teacher might quietly invite the student to take a deep breath together before discussing next steps. Research confirms that lowering stress and anxiety yields substantial gains for learning; Hattie (2023) reports an effect size of 0.81 for anxiety reduction. Hammond (2025) and Lemov and colleagues (2022) likewise emphasize that teachers' calm and steady tone reestablishes psychological safety and dignity. When teachers intentionally slow both their pace and their speech, they model the very regulation they seek to foster in students.

Offer a Small Reset Opportunity

Sometimes the smallest shift can help students regain emotional balance and refocus on learning. Offering a quick "reset" signals support, not discipline. It's comparable to a Ctrl-Alt-Del reset: interrupting the emotional freeze so the student can regain control and continue. A teacher might quietly say, "Do you need a short reset before we continue?" and give the student a calm option—such as taking a sip of water, changing seats, stretching at the back of the room, or simply closing their eyes for a few slow breaths. These brief, low-stakes choices restore self-control while keeping the focus on learning (Bailey, 2021; Bilmes, 2012; Sprick et al., 2021).

In preschool or early elementary classrooms, resets might include watering a class plant, passing out papers, or offering a squeeze ball or soft fidget. A middle school teacher might casually hand a student a piece of sugar-free gum—something novel that interrupts frustration with humor and novelty—while a high school teacher might suggest, "Grab a drink, walk to the back, and come back when you're ready." These gestures communicate care and confidence in the student's ability to self-regulate.

PBIS (2022) and Sprick (2021) describe these resets as Tier 1 and Tier 2 supports—short interventions available to everyone (Tier 1) or targeted to individual needs (Tier 2). Hammond (2025) connects such opportunities to stress recovery: small movement or sensory changes allow the brain to downshift from threat to focus mode. Similarly, Hattie (2023) notes that classroom climate and self-regulation have substantial effect sizes (0.52–0.75), underscoring that emotional balance directly impacts learning. Saphier and colleagues (2025) and Noddings (2013) reinforce that calm, relational responses preserve dignity and a sense of belonging, helping students feel safe to rejoin the group.

Offering a "reset moment" is less about discipline and more about restoration. Whether it's handing a student a water bottle, inviting them to walk a note to the office, or even offering a mint or piece of gum to break the tension, the message remains the same: *You're safe here. Let's start fresh.* These small, intentional choices cultivate emotional safety, mutual respect, and sustained engagement.

The following lists include additional quick reset strategies that have been recommended by teachers.

Sensory or Physical Resets

- **Trade a chair:** Allow the student to swap seats for one period (a stool, a standing desk, a floor cushion, or even the teacher's chair).
- **Magic marble:** Give the student a small grounding object such as a stone, marble, or coin to hold and return when ready.
- **Go get cold water:** A sip of cold water or holding a cool object can calm the body's stress response.
- **Stretch challenge:** Invite the student to stretch tall, reach for the ceiling, or move in slow motion to release tension.
- **Walk-and-reset pass:** Let the student take a quick walk or deliver a short note to the office to get moving and reset focus.

Cognitive or Humor Resets

- **Two truths and a fib:** Have the student share two true statements and one fib about a topic; the teacher guesses the fib to break the tension.
- **Trivia timeout:** Ask a quick, fun question such as "Would you rather explore the ocean or space?" to redirect thinking.
- **What song fits your mood?:** Let students identify a song that describes how they feel to promote self-awareness.
- **Alphabet challenge:** Challenge the student to name five animals, foods, or objects that start with a specific letter to redirect their attention.

Novel Sensory Breaks

- **Offer gum, a mint, or a sip of water:** Small sensory shifts, such as chewing or hydration, can lower tension and promote calm.
- **Choose your snack mascot:** Let younger students pick between two small snacks, such as crackers or pretzels, to reengage through choice.

- **Aroma reset:** Provide a lightly scented cotton ball (such as orange or peppermint) and encourage deep breathing to reset emotions.

Creative Expression Resets

- **Sketch a quick doodle of your mood:** Allow students to draw something that represents how they feel to externalize emotions.
- **Five dots:** Draw five random dots on paper and have students turn them into a quick picture or design.
- **Take a picture walk:** In digital settings, let students scroll through images of classroom projects or nature scenes for a short mental break.

Micro-Task Resets

- **Give a purposeful errand:** Assign a brief task, such as checking the pencil sharpener, organizing materials, or wiping the whiteboard.
- **Class helper of the moment:** Let the student take on a simple helping role like distributing papers, resetting technology, or watering a plant.
- **Minute of mastery:** Ask the student to teach or explain something they know well to reestablish confidence and engagement.

Routine, Moderate-Prep Strategies

Employ the 2×10 Strategy

Taking just 2 minutes a day for 10 consecutive days to engage a student in a personal, nonacademic conversation can dramatically improve trust, behavior, and classroom climate (Honsinger & Brown, 2019). This strategy, sometimes called 2×10, is grounded in trauma-sensitive and relational teaching practices: connection precedes correction, and consistent attention communicates care (Bailey, 2021; Bilmes, 2012; Hattie, 2023).

Angela once coached a secondary teacher who applied the 2×10 strategy with a particularly challenging student—a teenager who entered class each day angrily, muttering expletives, and slumping into his chair. Instead of reprimanding him, the teacher devoted two quiet minutes each day to a friendly check-in during the class's independent warm-up time. At first, the student's responses were brief, even dismissive. But by the end of the first week, he began to talk about his frustrations with school, admitting that his anger was not personal—it was about feeling disconnected and irritated by academics. Over the following days, their consistent conversations deepened.

By the second week, they reached an informal agreement: he would enter calmly and listen respectfully, while she would acknowledge his effort and continue checking in. Within a month, his demeanor changed; he began participating in discussions. Two years later, he returned in his Army uniform to thank her, sharing that those two-minute connections had marked a turning point—the first step in rebuilding his sense of purpose and belonging.

Such consistent, structured relationship-building efforts are supported by extensive classroom research. Lemov and colleagues (2022) describe this kind of intentional care as "dignity work," while Saphier and coauthors (2025) identify frequent positive teacher–student interactions as essential for maintaining classroom climate. Likewise, Noddings (2013) reminds educators that sustained, authentic attention to a student is an ethical act of care. Teachers who make a small but steady investment of time have a disproportionately large impact on student motivation and self-worth.

Teach, Model, and Reinforce Social Skills

Many classroom disruptions stem from students' lack of social or problem-solving skills rather than defiance. Teaching, modeling, and reinforcing how to disagree respectfully, listen actively, and resolve problems calmly give students constructive ways to handle frustration and conflict (Bailey, 2021; Bilmes, 2012; Sprick et al., 2021). A teacher might demonstrate how to say, "I understand your point, but I see things differently," and then have students role-play the skill during class meetings or cooperative projects. Research confirms that teaching pro-social skills yields substantial benefits for achievement and behavior. Hattie (2023) reports an average effect size of 0.48—well within the zone of desired impact—showing that explicit social-skills instruction merits consistent classroom implementation. Likewise, Noddings (2013) emphasizes relational care and empathy as essential classroom norms, while Saphier and colleagues (2025) note that teachers must model the interpersonal behaviors they expect of students.

Across grade levels, the approach can be adapted: an elementary teacher may teach turn-taking language during group work, whereas a secondary teacher might guide respectful debate using sentence stems that keep discussions civil. Hammond (2025) and Lemov and colleagues (2022) highlight that such routines build belonging and cognitive self-discipline, and PBIS (2022) and Sprick (2021) remind educators that modeling and reinforcement—acknowledging students when they use social strategies appropriately—help the behaviors stick. Teaching these skills intentionally transforms behavior management into relationship building and equips students with lifelong tools for being well-rounded human beings.

Use Self-Regulation Tools

Helping students manage their focus and emotions reduces disruptions. Tools such as projected countdown timers, self-monitoring checklists, and calm-down corners support students in self-regulating. Almost any approach to teaching students self-control (effect size = 0.66; Hattie, 2024) provides a significant return regarding academic and affective growth. For example, a student overwhelmed by group work can use a designated reflection space before rejoining the group. A 3rd grade teacher in California monitored group work, and when students were not productive, they were asked to move to the "reset table." The teacher accompanied the students and told them they had a specific amount of time (never more than three minutes) to make an adjustment and produce something of quality. The teacher set a quiet timer and returned precisely when promised. Most of the time, the student returned to the group with a piece of work to contribute.

The following classroom situation shows how a teacher's understanding of a self-regulation continuum tool can change both practice and outcomes. Marisol was a 5-year-old kindergartner attending school for the first time. During the first few weeks, she rarely spoke and often avoided group activities. Even small frustrations—such as tangled shoelaces or a tricky puzzle—could trigger tears, screams, or complete refusal to move. Although she seldom joined whole-group activities, songs, or center play, her teacher soon discovered in one-on-one moments that Marisol had understood nearly everything happening around her and she performed well on early reading and math assessments.

Still, the emotional outbursts were taking a toll on the classroom, and several colleagues urged the teacher to have Marisol evaluated for special education. Her teacher hesitated, sensing something deeper than disability. With guidance from her instructional coach, she used a five-stage self-regulation tool to reflect on Marisol's development. She realized that, while most of her students functioned at the higher levels of emotional regulation, Marisol was still at a much earlier stage, less regulated than most of her peers, but not outside the bounds of typical emotional developmental for pre-schoolers. Marisol was simply earlier on the continuum of learning how to name and manage big feelings.

Armed with that insight, the teacher shifted from reacting to behaviors to explicitly teaching self-regulation. She wove short "feelings check-ins" into daily routines for the whole class, modeled language for identifying emotions, and practiced simple calming techniques such as deep breaths and stretching. For Marisol, she added gentle coaching during transitions and guided her through short reset breaks whenever frustration appeared.

Within three months, Marisol—and several peers who benefited from the same routines—showed remarkable growth in managing emotions. Her meltdowns decreased dramatically, and she began participating eagerly in songs and group work. The other teachers working with Marisol now agreed that special-education testing was unnecessary. By recognizing where Marisol truly was on a fairly simple five-stage self-regulation tool and responding with targeted instruction instead of a referral, the teacher helped her build skills that would last well beyond kindergarten.

Follow Up Later

Conflicts aren't always resolved immediately. Following up later allows both the student and teacher to reflect and repair the relationship. Checking in one-on-one with the student reinforces the idea that the goal is long-term growth rather than punishment (Young, 2025). In an elementary setting, this might sound like this: The teacher approaches a student late in the day and gently says, "Remember earlier when I reminded you to stop talking while others were speaking? I really love hearing your ideas, and I want everyone to have a chance to share. Next time, I need you to raise your hand. That way, we can all hear your great thoughts." In middle school, the conversation could look something like this: Once class wraps up, the teacher casually takes the student aside and says, "Hey, about earlier—I just wanted to make sure we're OK. Are we good?" After the student nods, the teacher smiles and says, "Awesome, thanks. Just remember, I'm here if you ever want to talk."

This strategy provides two significant benefits. It helps rebuild and strengthen student–teacher relationships (effect size = 0.57) and serves as constructive feedback (effect size = 0.50; Hattie, 2024). The elementary example illustrates that the teacher offers specific feedback to guide future behavior and that they work on relationship repair. In the secondary example, the teacher primarily focuses on relationship repair.

Empower Students with Choices

Providing students with structured choices helps them feel ownership over their learning, which increases engagement and decreases resistance (Bailey, 2021; Bilmes, 2012; Jensen, 2019). Even simple options—such as choosing between two assignments, deciding how to demonstrate understanding, or selecting a partner—can turn compliance into cooperation. Student autonomy is strongly linked to intrinsic motivation and achievement, with choice showing a mean effect size of 0.40 in Hattie's global research database (Hattie, 2023).

Consistency is key: the *regular and deliberate use* of offering two or more clear, equal-value options builds decision-making skill and emotional regulation over time (PBIS, 2022; Saphier et al., 2025; Sprick et al., 2021). In preschool and early elementary settings, a teacher might say, "Would you like to use crayons or markers for your story picture?"—keeping both options acceptable. In middle school, a teacher could ask, "Do you want to work on the summary first or the reflection paragraph?" In high school, it might sound like, "You can collaborate with a partner or complete this analysis independently—your choice." Each version keeps expectations firm while granting agency.

Across grade levels, predictable choice-making routines promote self-direction, confidence, and collaboration. Hammond (2025) emphasizes that structured autonomy develops *learning power*—the belief that effort and strategy determine success—while Sprick (2021) notes that offering choice often prevents defiance by preserving student dignity. When teachers build this pattern of shared decision making into daily practice, they strengthen students' ability to take initiative and manage themselves, hallmarks of both effective instruction and positive classroom climate.

Use Consistent Questioning

Helping students think through their own actions can guide them toward correcting behavior independently. Rather than calling students out publicly, effective teachers use a calm, private sequence of three reflective questions—always in the same order:

1. What are you doing right now?
2. What should you be doing instead?
3. What can you do to change that?

It's the consistent use of this exact three-question sequence—and the repeated practice over time—that drives the strategy's success. When students hear the same pattern in the same tone, they begin to internalize it, eventually asking themselves these questions before the teacher needs to intervene (Bailey, 2021; Bilmes, 2012; Saphier et al., 2025; Sprick et al., 2021).

In early grades, the teacher might gently whisper the questions to help a child redirect mid-task. In middle or high school, the same sequence can be delivered with brief eye contact and a calm tone, signaling accountability without confrontation. Over time, this repeated dialogue becomes a form of cognitive coaching. Hammond (2025) calls this process "meta-strategic thinking"—teaching students to monitor their own behavior and make better choices. Similarly, Hattie

(2023) identifies self-judgment and reflection (effect size = 0.81) and metacognitive strategies (effect size = 0.58) as two of the highest-impact factors on student learning and self-regulation. When used consistently and respectfully, this questioning process moves students from dependence on external correction to self-regulation. It transforms discipline from something done *to* students into something done *with* them, nurturing both reflection and responsibility.

Clarify Expectations and Reinforce Them

Clearly stating and consistently reinforcing classroom expectations helps students understand what success looks like and how to contribute to a calm learning environment. Teachers might say, "In our class, we raise hands before speaking," and display brief, visual reminders to keep routines predictable. Setting expectations early and revisiting them often support both structure and belonging (Bailey, 2021; Bilmes, 2012; Sprick et al., 2021).

Consistency is just as important as clarity. When teachers uphold expectations for all students and model the same respectful behavior they request, they communicate fairness and trust. Saphier and colleagues (2025) note that modeling and consistent follow-through strengthen both authority and credibility. Hattie (2023) adds that teacher clarity—how well students understand the "what" and "why" of classroom expectations—remains one of the most significant contributors to achievement and engagement. In a kindergarten classroom, this might mean practicing how to line up quietly with visual supports and positive reinforcement; in high school, it could involve establishing discussion norms like "one mic at a time" and respectfully redirecting off-task talk. Sprick (2021) and PBIS (2022) describe these routines as Tier 1 supports or "universal practices that build safety and predictability for all students." Lemov and colleagues (2022) similarly emphasize that clearly defined norms and follow-through reinforce a culture of dignity and shared responsibility. Maintaining consistency, avoiding interruptions, and modeling calm responses help expectations remain both clear and meaningful.

Teach Collaborative Problem Solving

Rather than stepping in to solve every conflict, teachers can help students work things out for themselves through clear, structured questioning. Simple prompts such as "Can you tell me what happened?" "How do you think your classmate feels right now?" and "What would be a fair way to fix this?" encourage empathy and accountability while maintaining calm and respect. This method—central to restorative and relationship-based classroom management models—teaches students to pause, reflect, and consider others' perspectives before acting (Bailey, 2021; Bilmes, 2012; Noddings, 2013). Teachers at a K–8 school in Colorado use this approach during community circles to address classroom or playground conflicts. The school maintains explicit community norms that every teacher reinforces daily. During "circles," students use this shared language—rooted in those community norms—to explain, listen, and suggest fair solutions. This consistent structure builds trust and reduces the need for adult arbitration.

Across grade levels, reflective questioning can sound different but follows the same purpose. In elementary classrooms, a teacher might guide two students in explaining their perspectives and agreeing on a way forward. In middle or high school, reflection might take place during an advisory circle or after a disagreement during a group project. Lemov and colleagues (2022) and Saphier and colleagues (2025) emphasize that dignity and structured dialogue sustain belonging and accountability, while PBIS (2022) and Sprick (2021) note that such student-led reflection helps prevent escalation and teaches lifelong interpersonal skills. The underlying message is that conflict isn't just managed; it's taught. When students learn to repair harm and restore relationships, the classroom becomes a more empathetic, self-regulating community.

Offer a Change of Space

Sometimes a student simply needs a reset. When emotions run high, guiding a distressed student to a calm, neutral area can help them regain composure and return to learning. A reassuring statement such as, "Take a break here. Join us when you're ready," communicates both trust and care. This reflective pause—central to many behavior and emotional-regulation models—gives students space to self-regulate without feeling punished (Bailey, 2021; Bilmes, 2012; Noddings, 2013).

Across grade levels, this practice looks different but serves the same purpose. In an elementary classroom, a teacher might have a "cool-down corner" with soft lighting or a feelings chart; in a high school setting, a quick trip to the water fountain or a few minutes to work independently away from a group task can serve the same purpose. PBIS (2022) and Sprick and colleagues (2021) describe these calm spaces as Tier 1 and Tier 2 supports—proactive systems used schoolwide (Tier 1) or in small-group or individual situations (Tier 2) to teach students how to regulate emotions before behaviors escalate. Research consistently shows that emotional regulation and positive classroom climate enhance academic engagement. Hammond (2025) emphasizes the need for attentional environments that reduce cognitive overload, while Saphier and colleagues (2025) and Hattie (2023) connect predictable, calm teacher responses to greater student trust and achievement. Offering a brief change of space is not about removal—it's about restoring readiness to learn and maintaining safety for everyone.

Encourage Self-Reflection *Before* Consequences

When a student resists direction, a short reflective pause may prevent escalation and build accountability. Rather than asserting control, the teacher shifts ownership back to the student by asking, "What do you need from me to get started?" This question—central to restorative and reflective models—invites students to problem-solve and regulate before consequences are considered (Bailey, 2021; Bilmes, 2012; Sprick, 2021). If the student replies with "Nothing," the teacher might calmly offer choices: "Do you want to take a break before starting this set of questions, or skip the first 5 and focus on 6 through 12?" Options such as these model self-management while maintaining expectations (Sprick et al., 2021; PBIS, 2022). In elementary settings, a teacher might say, "Would you like to begin the first problem with a partner, or do it on your own after a minute to breathe?" In a high school lab, a teacher might reframe defiance by asking, "What's getting in the way of starting the experiment, and what would help you move forward?"

This strategy aligns with research showing that metacognitive reflection (effect size = 0.58) and self-judgment (effect size = 0.81) strongly influence achievement (Hattie, 2023). Hammond (2025) calls these "meta-strategic moves," helping learners evaluate effort and emotion before acting. Likewise, Saphier et al. (2025) and Lemov and colleagues (2022) stress that reflection framed through dignity builds trust, while Bailey (2021) reminds educators to prioritize connection before correction. By guiding reflection first, teachers uphold authority without a power struggle and reinforce that discipline is an opportunity for growth, not defeat.

Conduct Conversations That Coach

Instead of reprimanding students or sounding like a broken record, many teachers use coaching strategies to guide behavior and academic improvement—and it works. Two high school instructional coaches from suburban Chicago were among the first to adapt the PDA (Positive Descriptive Appreciation) and Mini-Reflect for use with students. Both tactics are found in *The Instructional Coaching Handbook* (Young et al., 2023). After being trained in coaching teachers, they realized the same respectful, thought-provoking approach could be just as effective with students.

These conversations start with a PDA conversation, where the teacher names a specific strength and then asks the student to reflect on how they achieved that outcome. If a small issue needs attention, the teacher can pivot to a Mini-Reflect conversation, which identifies a missed opportunity, opens a brief problem-solving dialogue, and ends with a simple plan.

Here's what the steps look like in practice with a high school student named Neto:

- **Positive Descriptive Appreciation**
  1. Start by labeling the student's success: "Neto, you always engage with the material enthusiastically in class. You bring energy into the room."
  2. Follow up with a question: "What helps you get into the lesson so quickly?"
  3. After the student responds, connect it to a broader focus: "That kind of engagement is exactly what we're aiming for with active learning across the school."
  4. Encourage continuation: "Keep it up—your energy really sets the tone for the room."

- **Mini-Reflect**
  1. Move to a Mini-Reflect if there's a minor issue: "I've noticed you're late almost every day. What's going on?"
  2. After the student shares, help brainstorm solutions: "What might help you get to class on time?"
  3. Guide the student to commit to a plan: "How about setting a watch alarm as a reminder?

4. Plan to revisit the issue in a few days or a week. "Let's try that, and you and I can check in next week about how it's working."

5. Have the student summarize the conversation: "Can you recap our plan?"

These kinds of conversations help students feel seen and supported, not scolded. They're simple, brief, and highly effective for both academic and social-emotional moments. In student surveys, feedback has been overwhelmingly positive; students say they don't feel like they're in trouble or being hassled—they feel genuinely supported and helped.

Long-Term, High-Prep Strategies

Plan for Student Triggers

Many behavioral disruptions are predictable. Transitions, group work, and unstructured time often trigger student anxiety or resistance. Teachers can anticipate these moments and provide structured choices and warnings to help students prepare; this type of careful planning is part of effective classroom management (effect size = 0.44; Hattie, 2024). For instance, before moving students into pairs, we heard one teacher say, "In about five minutes, we'll start working with partners, so think about who you'd like to pair up with." Giving students this kind of heads-up helps them mentally and emotionally prepare for the change. Another great benefit is that students who struggle with impulse control may benefit from alternative participation options, such as being assigned a structured role in a group or using cue cards to communicate during discussions.

A middle school teacher in Phoenix who enjoyed learning new strategies but knew that sometimes change was difficult for her students developed a clever method to prepare them. She had them line up outside the classroom on a day she was introducing something new and took time to explain the strategy and why she had decided to use it. She always had new materials on students' desks and made sure they were ready for them, letting them know what they would find there. She asked for questions and comments. She said that, at first, students didn't respond much, but after several of her new strategy lineups, the students became more comfortable and willing to speak up about the changes. She also gave them a specific time limit for the trial. For example, she said, "We are going to try this strategy for the month of February. At the end of the month, you'll get your evaluation form to let me know how or if the strategy has affected your learning." The students responded enthusiastically to being able to evaluate what was happening in their classroom.

Establish and Teach Norms and Routines

Structured environments help students feel safe, reducing anxiety and preventing misbehavior (Hattie, 2023; Saphier et al., 2025). When teachers co-create norms with students, regularly reinforce expectations, and practice routines without the pressure of academic tasks at first, they establish a strong foundation for positive behavior. Quick, engaging activities such as friendly competitions can make transitions smoother and more enjoyable. Explicit norms and routines, especially around transitions, significantly support effective classroom management (effect size = 0.43; Hattie, 2023).

At one K–8 school, staff dedicated significant effort to establishing explicit norms and routines throughout the school year. After experiencing a particularly challenging semester, they realized students struggled with consistently demonstrating respectful behavior toward peers and adults. Teachers recognized the need to build civility within their school community. During their professional development sessions, teachers explored ideas around civility based on work by Brené Brown (2017) and Zaretta Hammond (2015, 2025). Both authors highlight how essential it is to speak honestly and respectfully, without making others feel dismissed, and how crucial it is to build classrooms that welcome and affirm everyone.

With this inspiration, the staff first came up with meaningful norms for themselves: "Try hard to understand others' viewpoints." "Talk directly but respectfully through conflicts." "Always keep sensitive conversations private." Next, teachers asked students to help create practical classroom guidelines, including things such as "Pay close attention when someone else talks," "Show respect even during disagreements," and "Encourage your classmates." Because teachers regularly reminded students of these expectations, they soon became second nature in daily classroom interactions. By the following fall semester, culture walks and student and staff surveys revealed clear evidence of civility, respect, and mutual support embedded in everyday interactions across the campus, leading to a noticeably improved school climate.

Address the Causes of Misbehavior

When a student repeatedly misbehaves or struggles with appropriate behavior, effective teachers become behavior detectives. Instead of labeling the student as problematic, the teacher asks, "Why might this behavior be happening?" It's much like reading a fuel gauge: behaviors signal a need, not a flaw, allowing the teacher to plan support rather than react with frustration. Through a process often called Functional Behavior Assessment (FBA), teachers gather information to figure out what triggers the behavior and what the student gains from it (PBIS, 2022). This proactive approach to decreasing disruptive behavior empowers students socially and emotionally, creates a calmer learning environment for both teachers and classmates, and potentially enhances academic performance (effect size = 0.82; Hattie, 2024).

For example, if a student frequently calls out in class, the teacher observes when and where it happens—perhaps noticing that it mostly happens during independent work (trigger) and results in the teacher's attention (outcome). Once the teacher understands the real issue, they can make a practical plan to help the student, such as modeling better ways to ask for help or changing aspects of the classroom environment to avoid problems. It's a bit like realizing a plant's leaves are turning brown from too much sunlight. Instead of just clipping off the dead leaves, you move the plant somewhere shadier. In practice, an FBA might involve tracking the behavior over a week, talking to the student and other teachers, and then creating a plan (with counselors or special educators) that could include changes such as giving the student short breaks between tasks or a signal to quietly request help. Consequently, teachers can implement interventions that genuinely address the root cause, helping the student learn better behaviors and reducing frustration for everyone in the classroom.

Behavioral challenges and mental health concerns are deeply intertwined. Managing a classroom isn't just about keeping students quiet or on task; it's really about creating a place where students know they're valued, cared for, safe, and encouraged to grow. When teachers use these strategies consistently, they can build classrooms that cut down on disruptions and strengthen students' emotional skills, trust, and genuine connections—even when it feels like an uphill battle. By making small, intentional changes each day, teachers can transform their classrooms into spaces where every student—no matter their struggles—can grow, thrive, and succeed.

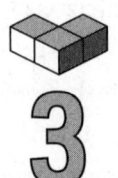

3

Academic Learning Gaps

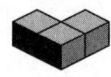

Long-Term, High-Prep Strategies

This chapter looks at school performance gaps—a common challenge that's become even more apparent in today's classrooms. Readers will find practical ways to spot exactly where students are struggling academically by using tools such as quick diagnostic checks and structured support. These strategies make it easier to provide personalized help, giving each student what they need most. The teaching and learning methods introduced in this chapter fit naturally into daily lessons, making them simple for general education teachers to use with all types of learners.

Packed with more than 65 instructional approaches, this chapter shows exactly how to close knowledge gaps and keep every learner moving forward. Some overlap between strategies discussed here and those covered in Chapter 4 are intentional. We'll highlight these strategies as they arise, marking relevant tactics and explaining their significance. Also, the strategies in this chapter fall into three groups according to the preparation and effort required for implementation:

- Immediate, Low-Prep Strategies
- Routine, Moderate-Prep Strategies
- Long-Term, High-Prep Strategies

Immediate, Low-Prep Strategies

Use Formative Assessment

Monitoring progress and adjusting instruction is key to finding and filling gaps. Formative assessment is often misunderstood. Perhaps it should be called *informative* assessment, as its primary purpose is to inform the teacher of instructional successes and challenges. Formative assessment needs to include every student, be visible or clearly audible, and give the teacher a clear picture of which students are learning what the teacher intends for them to learn and which ones are struggling. Formative assessment provides granular data about each student's learning to determine the next best steps in instruction. Formative assessment is a powerful tool for closing learning gaps. It supplies the "small data" teachers need to ensure that all struggling students receive instruction that works for them (effect size = 0.50–0.95; Hattie, 2024).

Here are some examples of helpful formative assessment techniques, and Figure 3.1 clarifies some misconceptions about what formative assessment is and is not.

In a 4th grade classroom in Northern California, a teacher used formative assessment while teaching students to form and use prepositional phrases in their writing. After the teacher's modeling and students' practice finding prepositional phrases in grade-level writing, the teacher asked students to write their own sentences using a prepositional phrase on the whiteboard; they had two minutes. At the end of that time, all students raised their boards. The teacher quickly marked her laminated roll sheet with the symbols *, ^, or @ to record their level of mastery. She then asked students to join one of three groups. The * group returned to a table with her while the others worked semi- and entirely independently, writing with prepositional phrases. The ^ group received a list of phrases from which to choose, and the @ group used newspaper clippings to find phrases from a professional writer they wanted to use or adapt in their writing.

The group with the teacher sorted prepositional phrases that could be inserted into sentences meaningfully. After about five minutes of instruction and practice in the teacher's small group, one of the students said, "Oh, I get it! This is easy!" The student then told the teacher, "You can go ahead and help the other groups. I can teach this one!" Within another five minutes, all the students in the * group who had initially struggled joined one of the other two

Figure 3.1   What Is Formative Assessment?

Formative Assessment Is Not...	Formative Assessment Is...
Choral response (without teacher feedback or analysis).	**Paired responses** in a setting, such as a small group, where the teacher can hear every response and adjust instruction accordingly.
Thumbs up, sideways, or down to assess how students feel about their learning. Similarly, students may be asked to raise their hands or nod if they understand the concept or skill.	**Thumbs or other hand signals** to answer a specific content-based question, for example: "Would describing the character as self-absorbed be accurate (thumbs up), somewhat accurate but incomplete (thumbs sideways), or inaccurate (thumbs down)?" This approach is followed immediately by students explaining or writing their reasoning.
Randomly selecting students by pulling Popsicle sticks with their names written on them to answer a question, while most students remain passive and do not engage in responding.	**Ensuring every student responds** by using whiteboards, paper, or digital tools that allow the teacher to see and review all answers in real time to adjust instruction as needed.
A quiz that is graded but not used to adjust instruction.	**A quick quiz** where the teacher uses results to immediately (that same day or the next) adjust instruction and potentially pull a small group for targeted support.
Exit tickets that are collected but not used to inform or modify the next lesson.	**Exit tickets that are reviewed before the next lesson** and used to address misunderstandings, modify groupings, or adapt learning strategies later that same day or during the next lesson. For example, if several students struggle with a math concept, the next lesson begins with a brief reteach before moving forward.

groups because they had grasped the concept. Before the end of the lesson, all students were using the news clippings to enhance their writing. The learning gaps regarding prepositional phrases had vanished from an intervention that took about 10 minutes and occurred during the lesson, not some other time of the day or week.

For further information on formative assessment, check out the strategies in Chapter 7.

Give Frequent, Specific, and Actionable Feedback

Give students timely and clear responses they can act on right away. Good feedback isn't just a teacher pointing out mistakes; it's a two-way conversation that helps students really understand and learn better (Biggs et al., 2022; Hattie, 2023; Saphier et al., 2025). When students' thoughts, confusions, or self-reflections are listened to carefully, the teacher can shape their feedback in ways that help students make sense of their guidance and put it into practice. Figure 3.2 includes examples of specific, actionable feedback.

Make Feedback Interactive

Some students pull back when they hear the word *feedback*, especially if they've come to associate it with being wrong or falling short. Maybe past experiences made it feel more like criticism than support. One way to shift that response is by making feedback feel like a normal part of learning—not a surprise or a punishment, just part of how we get better. Keep it specific. Keep it consistent. Turn feedback into a back-and-forth conversation. When students have a voice in the process, they're more likely to think about it, take it seriously, and use it to improve. A feedback-rich classroom fosters student engagement, builds growth mindsets, and leads directly to more substantial learning outcomes. Here are a few ways to make feedback more interactive and meaningful for students.

Figure 3.2   Specific and Actionable Feedback

Specific and Actionable	Not Specific and Actionable
Your ideas are strong; let's make your wording strong as well. You have used the word "good" five times in this paragraph. Go back and use our specific adjective lists to make your writing more vivid.	Your writing is not vivid. Use more adjectives.
Your first two steps are correct. Can you talk me through Step 3?... Ah, go back to your notes and look at the section on.... I will be back in a few minutes to check on how you're doing.	Your answer to question #2 is wrong; use your notes.
Your conversations were mostly clear, but each of you used the subjunctive incorrectly. That is probably because it is quite different than in English. Let's work on a few sentences together to make sure you have mastered that.	8/10 points on your conversation; you need to talk more.

- **Engage students in the feedback process.**
  - > Before reviewing student work, ask students directly where they need feedback.
  - > Prompt students to reflect on previous feedback before starting new tasks, guiding their improvement.

- **Make feedback ongoing and embedded in instruction.**
  - > Offer immediate, real-time feedback during class discussions, group activities, and individual tasks—not just after assessments.
  - > Regularly integrate teacher–student conferences, peer feedback sessions, and self-reflection so feedback becomes a continuous conversation, not a single event.

- **Listen to student responses to feedback.**
  > Encourage students to articulate their understanding and thought process in response to feedback rather than just fixing errors.
  > Use reflective, open-ended questioning techniques, such as "How do you interpret the feedback you received?" "What will you do next, based on this feedback?" and "Can you show me exactly how you applied this feedback?"
- **Ensure feedback is timely, specific, and actionable.**
  > Give feedback promptly, at a time when students can use it to improve their current work.
  > Provide straightforward, precise suggestions students can apply immediately. For instance, instead of vague guidance like "Improve your argument," say, "Your argument is strong; consider adding a counterpoint in the second paragraph to make it more persuasive."

Clarify the Learning Route

Imagine getting into a car and telling your GPS, "Let's go," without a destination. Starting a lesson without a clear objective is just like that—it leaves students uncertain about their direction. Your GPS needs extra details to prepare the best route (e.g., if slower surface streets are preferred over a freeway, the driver wants to avoid tolls, or the car is running low on gas and needs to fill up), anticipates confusion, and signals critical turns ahead (e.g., "Stay in the left lane, then make a quick right"). Learning objectives serve the same purpose. Even with inquiry-based lessons (less explicit instruction), students need a clearly defined destination and guidelines for success, including key checkpoints along their learning journey. If they make a wrong turn? Like a good GPS, effective instruction recalculates the route without judgment, redirecting students toward their learning goals.

Reflect and Revise

Keep checking in on what's working and what's not. Adjust your strategies often to make sure no one's slipping through the cracks. High averages can be misleading; a few strong scores might cover up the fact that some students still aren't getting it. Always ask, "Who is learning what?" The answer to that question should move the teacher to look for strategies that include the brains of students who are not yet meeting expectations. "Big data" from state exams or even unit benchmarks may cause marginalized students to be forgotten; a class average may be above the state, district, or school average, while a handful of students fall far below the standard. Looking at individualized data is crucial to help all students rise.

A school in Arizona decided to use common planning time to look carefully at individual data. Teachers brought student artifacts without names and collectively separated them into piles of "exceptional," "above expectations," "at expectations," "approaching expectations," and "below expectations." One grade level had been widely celebrated for having test scores significantly above district and state scores, so the group was somewhat reluctant to participate in the data activities because they felt their scores already showed their students were high performers. However, the results surprised them.

Over half of their students scored in the top two tiers. Another 30 percent scored in the next two groups. What surprised them was that almost 20 percent scored at the lowest level: one in six students. Essentially, the top two groups "carried" the average. When they looked closely at the students in the lowest level, they found many commonalities across classrooms. They began to ask questions about their instruction and how they might work to move student learning forward. Their willingness to dig in and adapt their instruction inspired many other grade levels to do the same.

This kind of hands-on approach to looking at data can be especially helpful when supporting multilingual learners and students with special needs in a general education setting. By moving past class averages and focusing on how each student is growing, teachers can make smarter, more targeted choices that help everyone move forward.

Raise the Ceiling

According to John Hattie's (2023) *Visible Learning*, robust teacher expectations (effect size = 0.58) and strong teacher credibility (effect size = 1.09)—the extent to which students feel their teachers genuinely believe in their success—hold tremendous potential to enhance student achievement. A practical and powerful way to reinforce high expectations in your classroom is by adopting a strategy from Saphier and colleagues (2025): intentionally delivering three key messages to students every day for about four weeks:

- "This is important."
- "You can do it."
- "I'm not going to give up on you."

Express these messages naturally, using a personal language style, so they become authentic and meaningful. For example, an elementary teacher might encourage students by saying, "Learning to subtract is so important because we use it every day! I've seen how hard you've worked—I know you can do this. And don't worry, I'm right here with you; I won't give up on you!" Similarly, a high school teacher could reinforce these messages by telling students, "Mastering persuasive writing matters in everything from college essays to job applications. You're more than capable of doing this; I've seen your improvement. Remember, I'm not giving up on you, no matter how challenging it gets."

Consistently repeating these messages helps students internalize the teacher's belief in their potential. This approach is particularly beneficial for students with special needs and multilingual learners, who often benefit significantly from regular reminders that their work is valuable, that their teacher believes in their ability to succeed, and that consistent support is available. When these students feel supported, encouraged, and valued, they're far more likely to persevere and reach their full academic potential.

Routine, Moderate-Prep Strategies

Organize Reteaching Sessions

Schedule additional sessions for struggling students. Following formative assessment, as noted previously, struggling students need specific time for a "second chance." The second chance should not duplicate the initial instruction. Often, teachers introduce new manipulatives, encourage role-playing, conduct oral rehearsals, relearn parts of a concept, or receive new practice examples. Likewise, reteach sessions should not simply be drills practice or involve low-level thinking. Many teachers reserve about 10 minutes of the lesson to reteach in small groups. Some teachers also conduct a small-group intervention at the start of the next lesson while the rest of the class works on that lesson's warm-up.

It's important to recognize that providing extra time in a special education resource setting (outside the regular classroom) is not the same thing as offering additional instructional time with the same general education teacher who initially introduced a skill or concept. Reteaching—soon after the initial introduction of skills or concepts— proves crucial for students with disabilities or multilingual learners, as they may have gaps in foundational skills and need help addressing misunderstandings adjacent to the initial content presentation. Students may well need additional support from a specialist teacher outside the regular classroom, but *their first line of extra support should occur in the classroom with their regular teacher.*

Solicit Peer Assessment

When students assess and support one another, they should be precise, free of judgment, and not focus on grades. For example, students might look at their peers' papers only to check for proper capitalization. One student should read the other's writing and then go back and talk about where their partner was successful and where they had questions: "You capitalized all your sentences except one. See, all these letters are capitals. Can you tell me why this one is not?" Students should be carefully taught how to talk to and engage with one another when doing this. The truth is that peer assessment can be relationship-building or relationship-ruining. Structure and specifics can make it the former.

Use Scaffolded Learning Activities

Vygotsky (1978) introduced the notion of the Zone of Proximal Development (ZPD), which basically describes the skills and ideas students can grasp when they have just the right amount of help—before they're ready to handle things entirely on their own. In everyday teaching, that means figuring out exactly where students are starting from and then providing targeted scaffolds to help them gradually take the next steps forward. Effective scaffolding connects new learning to what students already know, making it easier for them to pick up complex ideas. Hammond (2015, 2025) emphasized that all students should become independent learners, yet marginalized students are often left dependent on the teacher due to a lack of appropriate scaffolding. Simply giving all students the same assignment or tools often leaves some struggling to engage, whereas overrelying on rote practice for struggling students prevents them from participating in learning that requires more complex thinking.

A common misconception is that students who struggle with foundational skills cannot participate in higher-order thinking. However, a student who struggles with decoding a reading passage can still excel in inference and comprehension when listening to a text read aloud. These students deserve opportunities for critical thinking while they develop their foundational skills. The following are examples of scaffolding in action.

- A high school literature teacher used multiple versions of the same novel to customize learning. Students who read significantly below grade level read a simplified version of the novel independently while they worked in small groups with the teacher on excerpts from the original, grade-level novel. During class discussions, these students made meaningful contributions and, as the school year progressed, gradually progressed toward reading more complex, grade-level texts.

- In an Arizona science class, multilingual learners explored the concepts of solids, liquids, and gases through visual supports. They sorted pictures into categories and used gestures, key vocabulary, and drawings to show what they understood. At the same time, monolingual students worked on annotating the science text. This setup gave all students a way to engage with the lesson that matched their learning needs and supported their growth right within their ZPD.

- A middle school math teacher uses multiplication and fact charts as a quick reference tool for students who have not yet memorized their multiplication and division facts. While students are still learning foundational math skills, these charts allow them to engage in higher-order math tasks, such as solving algebraic equations or word problems, while they work on their fact fluency. Often laminated and placed on desks, fact charts provide an accessible scaffold that supports learning while building independence.

Sentence and paragraph frames prove incredibly effective when used with careful thought. The aim is to help students actively engage with new language and ideas, not simply complete a fill-in-the-blank exercise. When frames are too frequent or overly structured, students can lose interest and become passive. The key here is not to over-scaffold but to offer just enough support to stretch students' thinking while helping them access the content. Figure 3.3 includes a few tips for using frames to support learning in meaningful ways. Note: Cloze notes (i.e., fill-in-the-blank notes closely related to sentence and paragraph frames) work best for beginning language learners or students with specific learning needs. They shouldn't be used as a general instructional strategy for all students.

By scaffolding effectively within students' ZPD, teachers can close learning gaps while keeping students engaged in complex, meaningful learning experiences. Scaffolding strategies are especially effective for helping multilingual learners and students with special needs thrive in general education classrooms. By using visual aids, simplified instructions, guided practice, and interactive learning, teachers make the content more approachable. These kinds of supports also give students more than just access—they give them a way forward. With the right support, students are more likely to stay with tough tasks, feel better about what they're learning, and gradually start to understand more challenging ideas.

See Chapter 4 for additional specific strategies related to visual aids and tools that support scaffolded instruction for students with disabilities or multilingual learners.

Teach Students to Take Scaffolded Notes

Teaching students how to take notes—not just assigning them—ensures students develop the skills necessary to process, organize, and retain information effectively. Many students struggle with note taking because they were never explicitly taught how to do it, yet teachers often assume they already know or will figure it out on their own. Without guidance, note taking becomes a frustrating experience rather than an effective tool for deep learning.

Figure 3.3 Tips for Sentence and Paragraph Frame Use

Use Frames When You Want to...	Avoid Using Frames That Are...
• Introduce new, complex concepts or vocabulary. • Encourage critical thinking and deeper understanding. • Support students in constructing responses using specific academic language.	• Overly scaffolded and only require minimal thinking. • The primary form of instruction for all students.
Examples of Effective Frames to Use:	**Examples of Overly Scaffolded Frames to Avoid:**
• *Shakespeare uses _____ in his writing to _____.* • *In this story, the author's central message is _____. Evidence of this message includes _____.* • *Cells restructure and replicate themselves through two main processes: _____ and _____.* • *Modern scientists rely on the work of _____ as seen in _____.*	• *Shakespeare uses rhyme _____ in his writing to make the reader hear _____.* • *The central message of this story is _____ because when others are _____, the main character is _____.* • *Cells restructure and replicate themselves through two main processes called _____, which is when cells divide, and _____, which is when reproductive cells are made.* • *Newton's work on _____ is essential because scientists _____ on it to learn more about _____.*

A group of middle school teachers in Virginia recognized this challenge when they discussed their students' difficulty taking useful notes. One teacher admitted, "Well, who actually teaches them? I know I didn't really learn how to take notes until I was in college."

Her honesty opened the conversation, and soon, others shared that their own experiences with note taking had primarily been through trial and error. They realized that while they all expected students to take notes, none of them actually taught students how to do it. This realization led them to take intentional action. They decided that note-taking instruction would begin in 6th grade and continue through 8th, with explicit scaffolding in place to support students' development.

The 6th grade team created differentiated note-taking templates tailored to various students' needs. Some students received blank templates to practice independently, whereas others received pages with margin notes reminding them of what they should be writing. For students who needed the most structure, the teachers provided framed templates with key terms and guiding phrases, ensuring that these students could still participate in class discussions without falling behind. The teachers also planned how to remove these scaffolds as students gradually became more confident note-takers.

As part of their approach, they introduced structured note-taking strategies such as double-column notes (where students adjust the column headings based on the topic) to prepare students for more complex tasks. For vocabulary development, they taught students to use the Frayer Model, a strategy that helps them define and contextualize new words. Instead of simply writing definitions, students folded paper into four squares and bent a corner down to create a diamond in the middle. This format encouraged them to engage with new vocabulary by recording definitions, examples, nonexamples, and visual representations (see Figure 3.4).

By explicitly teaching students how to take notes and gradually increasing the complexity of their note-taking tasks, these teachers ensured that students built strong, transferable skills rather than relying on trial and error. When students are taught to use note taking as a thinking tool rather than as a passive recording exercise, they become more engaged, retain more information, and develop the ability to process complex concepts independently. In addition, scaffolded notes benefit students with disabilities and multilingual learners as they provide structure, clarity, and support, and they help make ideas more accessible.

Figure 3.4 Example of Scaffolded Notes

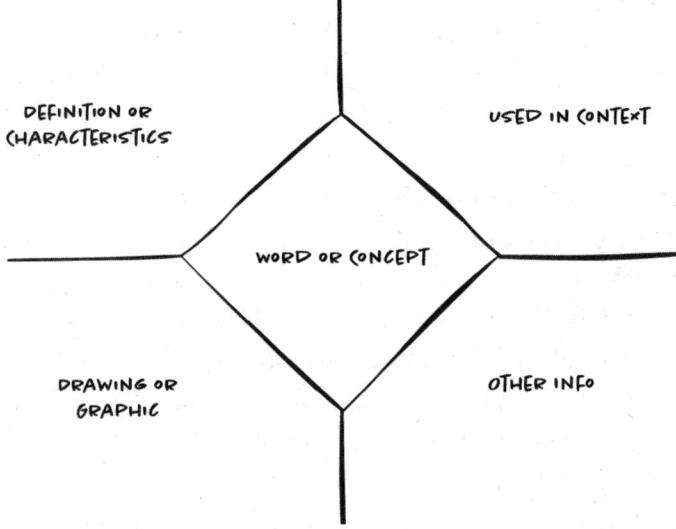

Use Spaced Repetition

Revisit content over time for retention (effect size = 0.62; Hattie, 2024). Remember to periodically bring previous learning back to the forefront of students' thinking. While planning lessons, think about the skills and concepts students will need and how long it has been since they studied them. Make the review fun and practical, allowing students to feel like they already have the knowledge they need for their new learning. Students who struggle with those previous skills or concepts should have a special learning time to renew before the whole-class review so they will feel "up to speed" with their peers.

Encourage the Use of Interactive Notebooks

Interactive notebooks are a great way to mix structure with creativity, making learning more engaging. For example, a middle school science teacher structured notebooks so one side had all the objective content (e.g., hypotheses, data, results). By contrast, the other side was for student reflections, diagrams, and real-world applications. The balance between structure and creativity kept students engaged and organized—and it even helped science students with special needs make impressive progress. Likewise, teachers in Hawaii embraced this concept—careful not to make it simply a "cut and paste" activity—and found great success. A math teacher had students do their homework in notebooks and annotate their thinking process as they worked. They were also required to add a real-world example or create an illustration or graphic for each skill set acquired. The teachers cut down the number of practice problems and concentrated on seeing how their students understood the math conceptually. Some teachers even made their exams "open interactive notebooks."

Start a Robust Vocabulary Program

Vocabulary instruction is critical to student success, and explicit word instruction fills the learning gap at both ends of the spectrum. It enriches high performers' learning and fills the void for struggling students. A simple place to start is with word walls. Think of word walls as a treasure chest that visually displays essential vocabulary with definitions, images, and sentences to help students anchor new words in their memory. These can be particularly powerful for multilingual learners; for instance, one bilingual elementary teacher used color-coded word walls featuring words in English alongside students' native languages, which helped students build meaningful connections to their prior knowledge.

Highly effective vocabulary instruction extends into multiple points of learning. We've noticed creative teachers focusing not just on definitions but on rich discussions, student-friendly explanations, and multiple exposures to words in varied contexts. Techniques such as using nonlinguistic representations (pictures or gestures), examples and nonexamples of word usage, and frequent interactive activities (e.g., Word Wizards, a playful game that rewards students for noticing and using vocabulary outside the classroom) deepen students' understanding and promote long-term retention.

Edit the Author is another game where students are challenged to come up with better, more precise words than the ones used in articles and books. Many classrooms highlight the Tier 2 vocabulary approach—explicitly teaching high-frequency academic words that students encounter across subjects (Beck et al., 2013; McKeown, 2019). For example, instead of teaching only content-specific terms like *photosynthesis* or everyday words like *tree*, teachers prioritize academic vocabulary such as *analyze*, *compare*, or *justify*, which are crucial for comprehension across disciplines.

Archer (2015), Beck and colleagues (2018), and McKeown (2019) all remind us that students need to speak, write, hear, and see vocabulary words to make the words part of their working vocabulary. Students often hear teachers use new words, but it is important to ensure students are actually using the words correctly in complete sentences and writing them in context. Figure 3.5 serves as a cue for the teacher to remember that students need to do all four actions— see, hear, write, and speak—to embed new words into their long-term memory.

Explicit vocabulary instruction is especially vital for special education students and multilingual learners. These students often face significant hurdles in vocabulary acquisition due to language-processing difficulties or limited prior exposure to academic vocabulary. Clear, structured, and repeated exposure to vocabulary—paired with visuals, gestures, and rich discussion—allows these learners to fully grasp new words, build their academic language proficiency, and achieve tremendous academic success. As Hattie's research (2024) confirms, intentional vocabulary instruction can potentially accelerate student academic achievement (effect size = 0.65). A high school art teacher at Nogales High School in Nogales, Arizona, found that posting realia for art terms near the class clock (because students were constantly looking at the time) helped her students acquire the language of art (Figure 3.6).

Figure 3.5 Student Use of Vocabulary

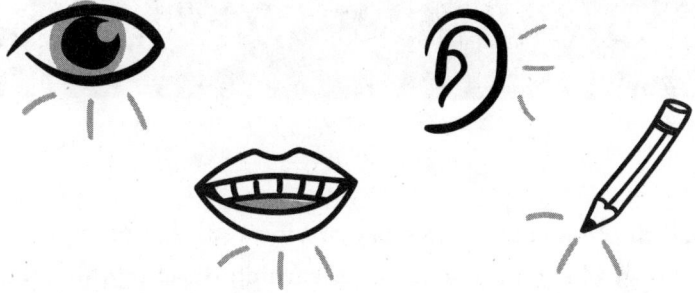

Source: From *The Instructional Coaching Handbook* (p. 94), by A. K. Young, A. B. Julien, and T. Osborne, 2023, ASCD.

Realize the Power of Peer Tutors

Pairing students strategically—for example, a stronger reader with a younger or struggling peer—can significantly boost reading skills and self-confidence. According to Hattie's extensive research (2024), this type of peer tutoring has a notable impact on student academic achievement (effect size = 0.66). A structured "reading buddies" approach not only improves fluency but also fosters meaningful connections, making learning enjoyable and motivating.

Figure 3.6   Vocabulary Displayed in Art

Judith often shares the story of Lily, a 9th grade student navigating dual challenges: a specific learning disability affecting her decoding and comprehension and the added complexity of being a multilingual learner still developing English proficiency. Recognizing Lily's struggles, her special education teacher introduced her to Julia, a patient and supportive older student, as a reading buddy. Initially hesitant, Lily nervously held her book, unsure of what to expect. Julia quickly put her at ease, gently guiding her through difficult words and offering enthusiastic encouragement at every small success. Over the next few weeks, Lily's confidence and fluency grew noticeably. She began to participate actively, asking thoughtful questions, making predictions, and engaging deeply in conversations about the stories she read. The turning point came when Lily finished a book, looked eagerly at Julia, and said, "I can't wait to read the next one!" This moment captured more than just improved reading; it revealed Lily's newfound love for books, genuine self-confidence, and the strength of a meaningful friendship. True learning is about feeling supported, encouraged, and empowered—and this type of peer tutoring provides exactly that.

Offer Extended Learning Time

Sometimes, regular class time simply isn't enough. Offering extended learning opportunities—before class, after school, or even within small portions of the regular classroom schedule—can significantly help students who need extra support or additional practice. Short, focused sessions (of 10–15 minutes) can effectively address specific skills or clarify misunderstandings in small groups or one-on-one interactions. In a practical K–12 classroom setting, teachers often build in brief reteaching segments during independent practice or seatwork. For instance, after the initial lesson, while most students move on to practice independently, the teacher might pull aside a small group of students who need extra help and provide focused instruction without disrupting the overall class flow. Some teachers also open their classrooms 10–15 minutes before school begins or offer a brief afterschool session once or twice per week, giving students regular and predictable opportunities for support.

Extended learning time is particularly beneficial for special education students and multilingual learners, who often process information differently or more slowly than their peers. For example, students with specific learning disabilities may experience challenges interpreting or applying new information, requiring extra minutes of direct instruction and guided practice. Multilingual learners might need additional time to translate mentally or clarify vocabulary and language structures. Providing brief but regular extended learning periods ensures these students get the extra support and processing time needed to build confidence and successfully grasp new concepts.

See Chapter 4 for additional strategies that support time flexibility and student pacing.

Long-Term, High-Prep Strategies

Engage in Task Analysis

Break down complex tasks into manageable chunks. Learning new material is a complex venture; students must see the task in discrete, achievable steps. Liken it to getting a child to clean a very messy room. If told, "Go clean your room," a child may often get sidetracked by a book on the floor and begin to read. Or they may grab a cuddly blanket and make a fort propped up with a Star Wars lightsaber from the closet. The chore is too vague and overwhelming to begin.

Instead, if told, "Let's make a list of what you will do and then number the steps. (1) Put clean clothes in the dresser and dirty clothes in the hamper. (2) Make your bed." If they receive clear steps like this, the odds are they'll persevere until the room is acceptably neat and the task is accomplished. With explicit steps and acknowledgment for tackling each step, the child is more likely to focus on the specific steps and overcome the enormity of the task. Students often hesitate or fail to begin a complex task in the classroom because the whole thing seems too much to grasp. However, if the task is broken into reasonable steps, the student can more easily begin. This tactic is akin to Hattie's (2024) description of success criteria and explicit instruction (both strategies provide an effect size = .64).

A group of high school math teachers in Oregon was distraught because their school was one of the highest performing in the state in all subjects except math. A few students were thriving in math, but a significant gap existed between those few and the rest of their classmates. The department asked Angela for help. She observed how the students were encountering math, and it was clear the teachers were all brilliant mathematicians; they knew their subject well, but students did not receive an opportunity to break mathematical concepts or procedures into parts.

Subsequently, as a group, Angela and the teachers spent time examining student work, considering the learning needs for the new topic, and determining discrete learning tasks for upcoming lessons. They were very introspective and had many "aha" moments as they worked together to determine the smaller pieces—steps, errors, misconceptions—of learning their students needed to address. After a few days of planning, they began instruction with new learning techniques for students to receive step-by-step procedures and frequent checks for understanding as they moved through the lesson. Halfway through one of the lessons, a student turned to a partner and loudly whispered, "I feel smart in math again!"

Conduct a 30-Day Experiment

Test intervention strategies over time. Conduct a 30-day experiment with targeted academic support for students performing below expectations. Provide consistent tutoring, teacher-led small-group instruction, sentence frames, math supports, and daily explicit and interactive feedback. This targeted effort can reveal the impact of high expectations and equitable practices on student performance. In addition, starting with only one or two students in a class may be more manageable than tackling the needs of all struggling students. Once you see success with one or two individual students, you'll have more confidence in arranging daily small-group interventions. This approach aligns with principles explained by Saphier and colleagues (2025), showing that consistent effort can significantly improve student outcomes.

Engage in Teacher-Involved Practice for Accuracy (TIP-A)

The key to building students' foundational skills is to guide them every step of the way, rather than wait to catch errors later. Teacher-Involved Practice for Accuracy (TIP-A) explicitly positions the teacher as an active participant during guided practice—not just standing back as students practice on their own. Inspired by John Hattie's (2023) emphasis on explicit instruction and work from both Archer (2015) and Groshell (2024) on clear, structured teaching practices, TIP-A helps students gain confidence and proficiency through careful, step-by-step teacher involvement.

Think about teaching a child to swim. First, you hold them in the shallow end. Next, you help them float with less support. Eventually, they swim independently. Similarly, TIP-A uses this gradual-release approach, but the teacher remains actively involved at each step, closely observing student progress and jumping in immediately to address mistakes. This proactive involvement lets you see which students need extra help or clarification before minor errors become significant setbacks.

Teachers in one New Mexico elementary school regularly use TIP-A in their classrooms. They combine explicit modeling with immediate checks for student understanding. They compare TIP-A to giving a dance lesson; you demonstrate each step, carefully watch students as they try it, and pause frequently to reteach any movements they haven't mastered yet. Depending on student needs, TIP-A can happen in whole groups, small groups, or individually.

A 5th grade teacher recently used TIP-A to help students distinguish between the literal meaning of the text and the themes of Kate DiCamillo's *Because of Winn-Dixie*. After first modeling her thinking with a short story the class had read the previous week, she reminded students that the literal meaning includes what happens, whereas the theme is the big idea or lesson the author wants us to take away. She read aloud a short excerpt in which Opal, the main character, lists 10 things about her mother, then she asked pairs to talk through what happened and what it might mean.

As students shared their ideas, the teacher noticed most pairs were accurately identifying events (e.g., "Her mom liked to plant flowers" or "She left when Opal was 3") but couldn't move beyond retelling to infer a deeper theme. Sensing the pattern, she paused the class and said, "I'm noticing something important. We're all getting really good at remembering what happened, which is great. But right now, I want us to stretch our thinking. Authors don't just tell us facts; they often want us to learn something bigger. Let me show you what I mean."

She reread the same passage and conducted a brief think-aloud: "So yes, Opal is remembering things about her mother, but why is this in the book? What's the author showing us about Opal? Maybe it's that remembering people we love, even when they're gone, helps us feel close to them. That's not exactly in the text, but it's what the text is helping us understand. That's a theme."

She then introduced a scaffolded sentence frame for the whole group: "The author is trying to show that...." Students turned and talked again, this time trying out new statements, such as "The author is trying to show that remembering someone can bring comfort" and "The author is showing how memories help us feel connected." When a few students still repeated literal events, she coached them live: "That's a great start. Now ask yourself, 'Why might that matter to the character? Why did the author include that moment?'" She also referred to an anchor chart in the room to show examples of literal versus thematic responses, and students practiced with a new passage. By the end of the lesson, nearly all students could use the sentence frame accurately and distinguish between literal meaning and inferred theme. The teacher described the shift as one of her strongest uses of TIP-A: "When I realized they were stuck, I didn't move on. I moved in."

Use Gradual Release to Build Independence

Hattie's research (2024) underscores the power of explicit teaching strategies, such as guided practice, to accelerate student learning (effect size = 0.64). Angela and Keith delineated the following four strategies during their work with WestEd to ensure students receive the right level of support at the right time.

Progressive Step Breakdown. One approach involves breaking complex tasks into smaller, manageable steps, allowing students to master each part before moving forward (adapted from Archer, 2015; Archer & Hughes, 2011; Groshell, 2024; and WestEd, 2016b). This explicitness is especially useful for multistep processes in which early errors can snowball into later misunderstandings. For example, when teaching multidigit addition with regrouping, a teacher might begin by walking students through each step in isolation: first adding the 1s column and stopping to verify accuracy, then addressing the need for regrouping, and finally adding the 10s column. As students become more confident, the teacher can adjust by combining steps, allowing students to take on more of the process simultaneously. Some students might need extra support in keeping track of regrouping, and others may be ready to complete problems with less guidance. The teacher can monitor student responses, either mentally or through written work, and use that information to identify who may need additional reteaching in a small group before moving to independent practice.

- Problem 1
  1. Add the 1s column. Stop. Explain why.
  2. Regroup if needed. Stop. Justify.
  3. Add the 10s column. Stop. Confirm.

- Problem 2
  1. Add the 1s column and regroup if necessary. Stop. Justify.
  2. Add the 10s column. Stop. Confirm.

- Problem 3
  1. Add the 1s column, regroup if needed, and add the 10 column. Stop. Verify.

Alternating Support. Another effective method alternates between teacher-led modeling and student-led practice (adapted from Lemov, 2021). This technique gradually shifts responsibility, ensuring students can process and apply learning before being expected to complete tasks independently. In writing instruction, a teacher might first model crafting an introduction for a persuasive essay while soliciting student input. Afterward, students collaborate to draft introductions while the teacher circulates and offers real-time feedback. Finally, students begin writing their introductions and applying what they learned. This approach allows for flexibility. If students struggle with an aspect of the writing process, the teacher can pause and return to a previous step for reinforcement before continuing. The teacher's role also shifts fluidly based on student progress, with instruction becoming more direct when necessary and less directive as students show readiness.

1. I lead, you assist: The teacher does a think-aloud and writes two sample introductions on the board while students take notes.
2. You lead, I assist: Students collaborate in small groups to write introductions for another essay while the teacher circulates, providing real-time feedback.
3. You do it independently: Students craft introductions on their own, applying what they've learned.

Gradual Removal of Instructional Aids. Keith and Angela were working with several teachers who only had visual representations of concepts they needed to teach (e.g., water table in science, welding symbols on a diagram, left and right political spectrum in history) when they stumbled on this notion of gradual removal of instructional aids (adapted from WestEd, 2016b). We often see this process in physical education. For example, when teaching a backbend, an instructional aide—such as a bolster or padded support—is initially placed beneath a student's lower back to provide full physical support. As the student gradually gains flexibility, strength, and confidence, the teacher progressively reduces the size or thickness of the bolster, offering less support over time. Eventually, the bolster is completely removed, allowing the student to safely and independently perform the backbend without any assistance.

In other subjects, teachers might begin with graphic organizers, sentence frames, illustrations, or step-by-step guides that provide a clear path for students to follow. For example, when teaching students to write a science lab report, a teacher might start with a highly detailed graphic organizer outlining each report section with guiding questions. As students become more familiar with the format, they transition to a simplified version with just the major headings. Eventually, students move toward writing the report with no structured support, relying instead on their notes and prior practice. This method ensures that scaffolding is removed at the right pace, preventing students from feeling overwhelmed while still encouraging independence. By observing which students still rely heavily on structured support, the teacher can determine who may need additional guided practice before moving forward.

1. Structured Phase: Students use a detailed graphic organizer to plan their introduction, methods, results, and conclusion.

2. Semi-Independent Phase: Students receive a simplified organizer with key headings only to encourage more independent thinking.

3. Independent Phase: Students draft the report without external support, relying on their notes and prior practice.

Tell, Ask, Remind. Archer (2015) and Archer and Hughes (2015) provide another spin on the gradual release of responsibility with "tell, ask, remind." This approach follows a structured sequence of teacher demonstration, guided inquiry, and independent student application. A teacher might begin by explicitly demonstrating how to identify and correct grammatical errors in sentences. After modeling, the teacher transitions to a questioning role, asking students to analyze new examples while offering verbal support. Finally, during independent or small-group work, the teacher provides light-touch reminders, reinforcing key concepts while allowing students to take the lead. Throughout this process, the teacher can adjust the level of guidance based on student performance. If students struggle with a particular type of grammatical error, the teacher can briefly return to direct instruction before resuming guided practice. Alternatively, if students demonstrate a firm grasp of the skill, the teacher can accelerate their transition to complete independence.

1. Tell: The teacher models identifying and correcting grammatical mistakes in a few sentences.
2. Ask: The teacher acts as if unsure and prompts students to help the teacher identify and fix errors in a few new examples.
3. Remind: As students work in pairs or independently, the teacher walks around, providing reminders and asking guiding questions rather than giving direct answers.

By carefully monitoring student progress, adjusting the level of scaffolding as needed, and identifying students who require targeted reteaching, teachers ensure that every student receives the support necessary to succeed. The ability to move back and forth between levels of guidance, rather than following a rigid sequence, allows instruction to remain responsive and flexible. In this way, guided instruction not only builds student confidence but also equips teachers with a structured yet adaptable framework for fostering independence in learning.

Create Personal Learning Profiles

Learning isn't a one-size-fits-all endeavor. Asking students how they prefer to acquire new knowledge in different subject areas and having them set their own goals give you information about how to move forward with each individual. Creating personal learning profiles for each student can be a game-changer for tailoring instruction. These profiles help students and teachers reflect on learning preferences, strengths, and improvement areas. When teachers use this information, they can customize their teaching to best support each learner. The idea is to help students take charge of their learning journey.

A school in Colorado had teachers go to their class roster and write everything they knew about each student as a learner. This work went beyond the typical labels students often receive, and educators were asked to think about what they had observed about how the students learned. They then sat at every student's desk to "see" the classroom as that student saw it. When they returned, the learning was tremendous. They created individual plans for students for their next lesson and shared them with the group. Strategies included rotating seat assignments, adding or subtracting scaffolds for students, creating more tactile and kinesthetic learning opportunities, and changing the time of day for some lessons. In addition, learning profiles prove valuable for students with special needs and multilingual learners since they are tailored to these students' unique strengths, challenges, and learning preferences.

Make Cross-Curricular Connections

Linking subjects strengthens understanding. When students encounter similar concepts across multiple subjects, their learning becomes more coherent, making it easier to retain and apply knowledge in meaningful ways. Cross-curricular connections help reduce knowledge gaps by reinforcing key ideas across different disciplines, ensuring that students who struggle in one subject can still engage with the material in another. Research suggests that interdisciplinary instruction fosters deeper understanding, leading to greater academic success, particularly for struggling learners (Hattie, 2023). Johnson (2018) outlines three phases of interdisciplinary teaching:

- Aligned: Teachers coordinate related concepts across subjects.
- Cooperative: Subjects intentionally collaborate to deepen learning.
- Conceptual: Students engage in fully integrated, theme-based instruction.

A 1st grade teacher aligned literacy and social studies by pairing the book *Last Stop on Market Street* with a unit on understanding community. This allowed students to connect literature to real-world concepts, reinforcing comprehension and social awareness. Likewise, a department of high school English teachers designed a cross-curricular unit on ethics and scientific progress where students read *Frankenstein* and *1984* alongside nonfiction articles about genetic manipulation. Simultaneously, the science curriculum covered genetic engineering, while social studies examined ethical and unethical technological advancements in history. This interdisciplinary approach brought together literature, science, and history, helping students explore how ethical choices shape scientific progress and profoundly influence society. In another high school, all freshmen were placed in schoolwide, cross-curricular teams where teachers collaborated to create thematic units across multiple subjects. As a result, student failure rates decreased significantly. Later, when given the option to return to traditional instruction, students overwhelmingly chose to stay in cross-curricular teams, citing a deeper connection to their learning.

By integrating subjects and making learning more interconnected, cross-curricular instruction bridges knowledge gaps, strengthens retention, and engages students who may struggle in one area but excel in another.

This chapter presents a collection of evidence-based strategies that help teachers close academic learning gaps by using assessment, feedback, and scaffolding to guide instruction. It shows how small, daily practices—such as formative checks, targeted reteaching, and structured note taking—build toward larger, long-term supports like personalized learning profiles and cross-curricular connections. Emphasizing clarity, repetition, and student ownership, this chapter demonstrates how thoughtful, data-informed teaching helps every learner progress from confusion to competence.

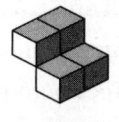

4

Special Needs in the General Ed Classroom

Long-Term, High-Prep Strategies

This chapter dives into what it really looks like to teach in classrooms where every student learns a little differently. Some kids need extra support, whereas others bring strengths that might not always show up on a test. The key is designing lessons that meet students where they are—lessons that make room for different skill levels, backgrounds, and ways of thinking. The more than 40 strategies in this chapter are for general education teachers to fully support students with special needs and multilingual learners in the general education classroom. There are natural overlaps with the strategies found in Chapter 3 for closing the academic gaps, which we'll highlight along the way.

The reader will also notice a theme in the approaches here; most have to do with "teacher clarity" of instruction:

- Learning organization
- Teacher explanations
- Guided practice
- Assessment of student learning
- Communication of the lesson goal, rationale, and precise performance expectations

Using these strategies together can speed up how quickly your students progress academically (effect size = 0.85; Hattie, 2024). This chapter also presents strategies—whole-group tactics, small-group strategies, and intensive individualized ideas—that are proven effective for students with special needs and multilingual learners. Additionally, we've arranged the strategies in this chapter into three distinct categories based on their complexity and the level of preparation required:

- Immediate, Low-Prep Strategies
- Routine, Moderate-Prep Strategies
- Long-Term, High-Prep Strategies

Immediate, Low-Prep Strategies

Use Specific Language and Maintain Teacher Clarity

Giving clear directions is a lot like setting the stage for a play. If the lights, props, and cues aren't in place, the actors can miss their entrances or forget their lines. By contrast, when everything's set up just right, students know exactly where to step in and what to do next. Clear guidance helps them stay focused, lowers frustration, and makes the whole lesson run more smoothly. Hattie (2024) points out how important it is for teachers to be crystal clear, showing that clearly stated directions and learning targets strongly boost student achievement (effect size = 0.85). Clarity becomes even more vital when teaching multilingual learners or students with special needs, who benefit immensely from explicit and direct guidance (Archer & Hughes, 2011; Groshell, 2024; Hughes et al., 2022).

Avoid vague directions, passive language, or overly general verbs—such as *learn, analyze, compare,* and other educational jargon—that leave students uncertain about specific actions to take. Instead, replace these unclear terms with active, concrete verbs that precisely describe what students should physically do, such as *reread, sort, underline, highlight, shade, write to explain, write to argue,* and *write to summarize.*

For example, rather than vaguely instructing students to "Work on the problems," directions should explicitly say, "Grab your pencils. Shade the fractions in problems 1 through 5 on page 23. Then write the matching fractions below each diagram." Clear, step-by-step instructions reduce confusion and help students stay engaged. In a 3rd grade class with multilingual learners, one teacher showed each step physically; used short, simple action words; and matched those words with clear gestures. She made instructions even clearer by having students say key phrases aloud, thoughtfully pairing kids together, and providing a set of numbered steps as they went along. These methods helped every student feel sure about exactly what to do and when.

Provide Rationale

Explaining why students learn something and how it connects to their goals helps students own their learning (Biggs et al., 2022; Hattie, 2023; Saphier et al., 2025). Students are much more motivated when they understand why they're learning something. It helps them see the purpose behind the lesson. When students see the connection between the lesson and their goals, learning from a task becomes a meaningful experience. A special education teacher in Arizona began a math lesson by explaining, "We're working on this project to help you use math for everyday situations and see why it matters." The students then explored real ticket prices for Arizona Diamondbacks games. Making that connection encouraged students to think more carefully about math and relate it directly to their own experiences.

One middle school science teacher Judith regularly observed was a pro at this tactic. He connected every single lesson to students' everyday lives. One day, he kicked off a lesson on the Bernoulli principle and air pressure by saying, "You might not know the name, but I bet you've felt it. Ever taken a shower and had the curtain cling to you the whole time? Raise your hand if that's happened." Hands shot up around the room. He smiled and added, "That's the Bernoulli principle at work. Let's dig into why that happens."

When students understand the *why* behind a task, a few important things start to click:

- **It feels purposeful:** Students can connect the work to their own lives or interests.

- **The goal is clearer:** Students know exactly what they're aiming to do.
- **Engagement increases:** Interest goes up, and students are more likely to dive in.
- **Thinking broadens:** Students start to reflect not just on what they're learning but also on why it matters.

Foster Students' Belief in Their Capacity

Helping students build confidence means offering encouragement that feels personal and meaningful to them, which is not always a simple task. Every student is different, so what lifts one up might not work for another. It takes time, attention, and a willingness to adjust along the way. However, when teachers understand how to show students they believe in their ability to succeed, students are much more likely to step up and meet those expectations. High expectations, paired with accountability, encourages students to take ownership of their learning and achieve at higher levels.

To communicate belief in capacity, a special education teacher in Maryland invites a college student with a learning disability to speak to the juniors and seniors in her classes each year. Her high school students must prepare to interview the college student with specific questions that are personally relevant. Consequently, the high schoolers get guidance and inspiration from someone with whom they can directly identify and recognize how that student has managed their learning disability and learned to be successful in college.

Here are a few simple ways for the teacher to help students build confidence:

- **Use growth-focused language.** Try to go beyond the generic "Good job." Try something like "I can tell this is challenging, but I see how hard you're working. Keep going; you're making progress."

- **Celebrate small steps.** Even the tiniest improvements may need recognition. Say, "I noticed you added more descriptive words this time. That's a powerful step forward!"
- **Promote a growth mindset.** Remind students that learning takes time. Say, "You might not have it down yet, but every time you try, you're getting closer."
- **Model what persistence looks like.** Let them know you've struggled, too. Say, "I had a hard time learning this when I was younger, but I stuck with it and eventually, it made sense."
- **Offer feedback that helps them grow.** Be specific about what to work on. Say, "Your argument is strong—if you include one more piece of evidence, it'll be even more convincing."

When teachers hold and communicate high expectations for student achievement, they directly lead to accelerated academic performance (effect size = 0.58; Hattie, 2024). When students hear specific, encouraging feedback and can see their own progress, it builds their confidence. Little by little, this shapes a classroom where progress is expected and students feel confident taking on tough tasks without backing down.

Provide Flexible Deadlines

The teacher can adjust deadlines for students who need support. Due dates should reflect the time it takes to learn something, not an arbitrary time limit. Adjust if students are engaged in their learning and take more time than initially expected. Limits are always a part of life, but we all expect some flexibility when we cannot succeed without more time. Set concrete goals with short-term deadlines so students don't get bogged down with the size of a task or fall into the trap of "doing it later" when the deadline is closer. A teacher who assigns a lengthy research paper needs multiple deadlines along the way—for both students with and without a formal diagnosis. After the first two days of research, a precise topic and thesis will be in rough form. From there, every goalpost is delineated (within a few days or a week at most) and checked.

Offer Visual Supports

Visual supports are powerful tools that use images, symbols, and graphics to enhance understanding, improve communication, and support learning. Creating visual or graphic organizers to display the relationship between course or subject content maintains the promise of considerably accelerating student academic achievement (effect size = 0.66; Hattie, 2024) by making abstract concepts more concrete, clarifying expectations, and reducing language barriers for all students. These tools are especially invaluable for multilingual learners and students in special education classes.

Graphic organizers provide visual scaffolding that helps students organize their thoughts, connect ideas, and retain information more effectively. They transform complex topics into manageable, structured visuals that promote deeper comprehension and engagement. The following are examples of graphic organizers and the thinking skills they support:

- **Concept maps** are structured diagrams that represent concepts as nodes and the meaningful relationships between them as labeled linking lines. They are typically organized from broad ideas to specific details, with cross links that show connections across branches. They help learners make thinking visible—organizing prior knowledge, surfacing misconceptions, and explaining how parts of a topic (e.g., stages, causes/effects, or systems) fit together. Figure 4.1 shows a concept map of mitosis that models how visual tools can organize and clarify key ideas in complex science topics.
- **Iceberg diagrams** illustrate the difference between what's easy to see on the surface and what's hidden underneath. The emerged tip of the iceberg represents the obvious facts

or surface-level details, and the larger part under the water symbolizes deeper meanings, hidden causes, or less obvious influences. For example, in a class reading of *Charlotte's Web*, the visible part of the iceberg might include facts such as "Wilbur is a pig" and "Charlotte is a spider." Beneath the surface, though, students discover deeper themes such as friendship, sacrifice, and courage, which aren't directly stated but must be inferred from the characters' actions, relationships, and what others say about them. Figure 4.2 shows how an iceberg diagram allows students to move beyond surface details to uncover hidden meanings, causes, and themes that lie "beneath the surface" of their learning while analyzing Robert Frost's poem "The Road Not Taken."

- **Venn diagrams** compare and contrast characters, events, or concepts.
- **T-charts** list pros and cons, facts and opinions, or causes and effects.
- **Story maps** help students sequence events in a narrative (e.g., beginning, middle, end).
- **Flowcharts** illustrate processes, such as steps in a math problem or historical timelines.
- **Hexagon cards** are labeled with key concepts, terms, or ideas, and students connect them to demonstrate how they relate or overlap visually. Figure 4.3 shows how a Minnesota English teacher used hexagon cards to prepare students for a literary analysis of *Macbeth*.
- **Bridge maps** help students visually show analogies or relationships between two pairs of concepts. This strategy pushes students toward deeper thinking because they have to explain clearly how the concepts relate to each other. For example, in an AP World History class, students might use a bridge map to illustrate relationships such as "Feudalism is to medieval Europe as the caste system is to ancient India." This exercise

requires students to clearly identify similarities between two distinct historical systems, helping them articulate and better understand complex connections. It also helps prepare students for their written products.

Figure 4.1   Example Concept Map

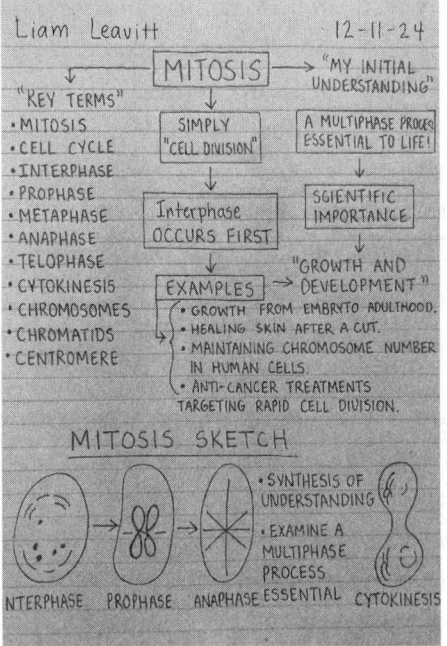

By incorporating visual supports into instruction, educators empower students to engage more actively with content, strengthen their understanding, and build confidence in their learning. Whether breaking down a complex science lesson or analyzing a story's structure, graphic organizers are versatile, accessible, and highly effective tools for all learners. However, teachers should recognize that completing a graphic organizer should not be the final destination of a lesson; it is merely a step toward deeper thinking and application.

Graphic organizers serve as valuable scaffolds that guide students toward broader goals, such as crafting thoughtful written responses, solving complex problems, or independently applying learned concepts. Just as construction scaffolding around a building eventually gets removed once the work is complete, graphic organizers should gradually be withdrawn, allowing students to demonstrate their thinking clearly and confidently on their own.

Figure 4.2   Example Iceberg Diagram

"THE ROAD NOT TAKEN"

- THE SPEAKER FACES TWO PATHS IN THE WOODS.
- HE CHOOSES THE PATH THAT APPEARS LESS TRAVELED.
- HE REFLECTS THAT TAKING THIS PATH HAS MADE A DIFFERENCE.

BENEATH THE SURFACE

- DECISIONS SHAPE ONE'S IDENTITY AND LIFE JOURNEY.
- THE TENSION AND UNCERTAINTY INVOLVED IN DECISION MAKING.
- INDIVIDUALITY AND THE COURAGE IT TAKES TO MAKE UNCONVENTIONAL CHOICES.

Figure 4.3   Example Hexagon Cards

Source: Used with permission from Molly Sutton Kiefer, Red Wing High School, Red Wing, Minnesota.

Routine, Moderate-Prep Strategies

Differentiate Instruction

Modifying teaching strategies based on students' readiness, interests, and learning preferences without compromising rigor or expectations of the original standards or texts increases all students' interaction with instruction. Differentiating instruction means tweaking teaching methods, giving students specific help where they need it, and providing different ways for students to show what they've learned—all without lowering standards or changing learning expectations (Saphier et al., 2025). For instance, rather than permanently substituting complex texts with simpler texts, many educators offer support to help all students access the same rigorous materials.

In a high school English classroom studying Shakespeare's *Romeo and Juliet,* students with reading challenges initially worked from a version with modernized language alongside the original text. The "simplified" text was a set of temporary steppingstones that enabled students to cross the river, even if they couldn't reach the bridge. This helped students clearly grasp the plot, characters, and main ideas so they could eventually dive deeper into Shakespeare's original wording. Over time, all students moved fully into using the original text, making sure that everyone could join in equally when the class discussed Shakespeare's key themes and how they connect to teens today.

At its core, differentiation just means being intentional. It means shaping instruction to fit the individual needs, strengths, and interests of each student. It can involve assigning different tasks, forming flexible student groups, approaching content in varied ways, or letting students move at their own speed through some activities. But the main goal is always to ensure equal access to learning—never to lower expectations. Deployed as described here, differentiation maintains the capacity to accelerate student academic progress (effect size = 0.58; Hattie, 2025).

Plan Flexibly

When students struggle, they need the teacher to slow down a bit, clarify explanations, and provide additional support in the form of visuals, simplified explanations, or interactive, hands-on experiences. Hattie (2024) highlights that flexible, responsive planning—continuously modifying instruction based on immediate student feedback—has the power to positively affect student academic achievement (effect size = 0.83). Quick check-ins, such as student polls or exit tickets, can give an instant snapshot of how well students are understanding the lesson.

For instance, in a high school history class studying civil rights, the teacher noticed signs of confusion and uncertainty during a whole-class discussion about key historical events. She paused the lesson to administer a quick-write, asking students to summarize their understanding of the content. Recognizing varied readiness levels, the teacher explicitly adjusted her approach. She grouped the more proficient students to examine primary source documents, annotating them with a few guiding, enrichment questions from their textbooks, while those who needed more foundational support used a simple, hand-drawn graphic organizer to summarize key events, people, and vocabulary from the era with the teacher. After this 30-minute differentiated activity, the teacher brought everyone back together for a whole-class discussion, which was much more robust and inclusive. As a result, all students accessed the same rigorous historical content and could meaningfully engage in analyzing the significance of important events in the civil rights movement.

Create Choice Boards for Engagement

Choice boards are a great way to offer students a variety of ways to show what they know, all while keeping things structured and purposeful (Culatta, 2023). When students are given options that connect with what they enjoy—like hands-on projects, thought-provoking challenges, or real-world applications—they're more likely to dive in and stay engaged. Figure 4.4 presents a sample choice board focused on fractions for upper elementary students, illustrating how teachers can offer students multiple pathways to demonstrate understanding through hands-on, analytical, and real-world applications. This type of visual support not only reinforces mathematical reasoning but also fosters autonomy and engagement by allowing learners to select tasks that match their interests and readiness levels.

Choice boards work especially well for multilingual learners because they let students pick tasks that match their language skills and comfort level. When lessons include visuals, real-life examples, or ties to students' cultural backgrounds, it makes complex math concepts easier to understand.

Figure 4.4 Example of a Choice Board

Hands-On Learning	Critical Thinking	Real-World Application
Use fraction tiles to build and label five different fractions.	Solve 10 fraction word problems, clearly explaining your reasoning.	Write a brief story featuring fractions used in everyday life, such as cooking or shopping.
Design a colorful poster that illustrates adding, subtracting, multiplying, and dividing fractions.	Compare 10 fractions and arrange them accurately on a number line.	Plan a pizza party for eight friends, detailing how to share three pizzas equally.
Use real objects (such as measuring cups, toys, or fruit slices) to demonstrate fractions visually.	Create and solve five original, challenging fraction word problems.	Find and explain five practical examples of fractions in your daily life.

Implement Flexible Pacing

Every student learns at a different pace, and flexible pacing helps ensure no one gets left behind or feels rushed. This approach is particularly effective in classrooms with many different types of learners because it allows teachers to adjust their teaching based on individual student needs. For instance, one middle school math teacher combined short video lessons, practice problems, and personalized support so each student could tackle algebraic equations comfortably, moving ahead only when they were ready. Those who needed extra time could take it, while others pushed ahead with more challenging problems. Research from Tomlinson (2017) confirms that flexible pacing boosts student engagement and understanding—making this a win-win strategy.

Think of flexible pacing like hosting a dinner party where each dish needs its own cooking time and special attention. Some dishes simmer slowly, whereas others cook quickly at high heat, and some dishes even taste better after resting. Just like a good host carefully coordinates every recipe so each one comes out perfectly, teachers use flexible pacing to manage learning carefully, ensuring every student gets exactly what they need at just the right moment.

Use Accessible Reading Materials

Making reading materials accessible is a powerful way to create a welcoming, supportive classroom for all students. Today's curricula and classroom tech offer plenty of ways to help all students connect with the content in a way that fits their needs. For instance, in a 5th grade science class, Judith observed that students learning about the water cycle had access to a digital read-along feature that supported their understanding as they followed along with the text. One student who struggled with reading fluency used the read-along and was able to follow the same content as the rest of the class but with extra support. Using headphones, the student listened to narration of the text while following the words on the screen. The digital version allowed him to adjust the text size and change the background color to something that made the material easier to read.

Features such as adjustable text, audio recordings, and digital versions allow students to change colors or fonts, accommodate students with reading difficulties, and enhance the learning experience for everyone. Where the curriculum or classroom technology provides the support, use the following:

- **Audiobooks** are perfect for students with visual impairments or reading difficulties.
- **Ebooks** allow for customizable font sizes, backgrounds, and contrast settings, which help students with visual impairments or learning disabilities (e.g., dyslexia).
- **Braille texts** are essential for blind or visually impaired students.
- **Text-to-speech software** reads text aloud and support students with dyslexia, with visual impairments, or who are learning the target language.
- **Bilingual texts** in both the target learning language and a student's native language support language learners and students with multiple needs.

Engage in Guided Reading

Small-group, guided reading instruction offers targeted support that helps students strengthen literacy skills through carefully matched instructional strategies. Recent research synthesizing two decades of evidence confirms that guided reading effectively promotes student fluency, comprehension, and confidence by addressing learners' individual reading needs (Morgan & Kuhn, 2023). Guided reading is all about working with small groups so teachers can focus closely on each student's reading strengths and challenges. It allows for support that's tailored to what each child needs in the moment. A teacher might help students break down tough words or lead an activity that sharpens their understanding of a text. With this kind of focused attention, students build vocabulary and start making deeper sense of what they read.

Think of guided reading as the work of a skilled music producer in a recording studio. Just as the producer listens closely to individual musicians, fine-tuning and adjusting each element—raising vocals here, softening drums there—to create perfect harmony, the teacher listens closely to each student and strategically adjusts their support. This fine-tuning helps every learner gradually strengthen their literacy skills and confidently master reading, achieving a powerful and harmonious result.

Scaffold Practice

Structuring practice so there is teacher support, peer support, and independent practice is beneficial for students with diverse needs; it provides the clearly articulated instruction necessary for high-needs learners. This approach is especially powerful for students with special needs who are included in the general education classroom, as it ensures they receive the right amount of guidance without being separated from their peers. For example, a student working on math fluency might first complete a problem alongside the teacher, then practice a similar one with a peer partner, and finally try one independently—building confidence and accuracy at each stage. This gradual release helps all learners, particularly those who require extra modeling or reinforcement, experience success and independence within the flow of everyday instruction. Even more detailed structures for scaffolded practice are found in these Chapter 3 strategies: Engage in Task Analysis, Use Scaffolded Learning Activities, and Engage in Teacher-Involved Practice for Accuracy.

Long-Term, High-Prep Strategies

Make Learning Contracts

Learning contracts are a great way to help students feel more in charge of their own education while also keeping them responsible. It's a bit like creating a personalized map for their learning journey—where the teacher acts as a guide and the student as the explorer. The contract clearly spells out goals, checkpoints, and expectations, but it also leaves room for adaptation if students encounter obstacles or need to adjust their path. Letting students help create their own contracts encourages independence, boosts motivation, and builds confidence—making learning more meaningful and transformative. Students develop problem-solving skills, resilience, and a deeper understanding of how they learn best by actively participating in their learning process.

Figure 4.5 illustrates an example of a student learning contract designed to strengthen reading fluency through goal setting, self-monitoring, and reflection. This sample, for upper elementary or middle school students, shows how individualized contracts can clearly define targets, learning strategies, and checkpoints while fostering student ownership and accountability for progress.

Utilize Accessible Technology

Accessible technology helps support learners with different needs by breaking down barriers to communication, learning, and participation. It includes specialized tools, devices, and software built specifically so that anyone, no matter their ability, can easily use technology. For example, screen readers are typically used by people with visual impairments, but they also help students with learning challenges or those learning a new language. A screen reader is a bit like having someone next to you guiding you through the online world—similar to how a ramp makes it easier for someone in a wheelchair to enter a building. Eye-tracking devices also help those with limited mobility "drive" a computer, just as a bridge allows someone on crutches to cross easily. These tools foster independence and create equal opportunities for people to succeed. Accessible technology, like a well-designed bridge, brings people closer to the same opportunities, enabling them to thrive academically, socially, and professionally.

Figure 4.5   Example Learning Contract

Learning Contract: Improving Reading Fluency

1. **Name:** _____   Grade/Level: _____
   Instructor/Mentor _____   Date: _____

2. **Learning Goal:** This contract is to improve reading fluency by focusing on accuracy, speed, and expression while reading aloud. My goal is to "Increase reading speed to at least _____ words per minute by (date).

3. **Learning Strategies:** To achieve the goal, I will:
   a. Practice reading aloud for at least _____ minutes daily.
   b. Use finger tracking or a reading guide to maintain focus while reading.

4. **Evidence of Learning:** I will demonstrate progress in reading fluency by:
   a. Recording and comparing a baseline reading fluency assessment with later recordings.
   b. Completing weekly timed reading passages and tracking improvements in words per minute.

5. **Support & Resources:** To help me succeed, I will use:
   a. Books at or just above my current reading level.
   b. Audiobooks and read-along materials to model fluent reading.

6. **Timeline & Milestones:**
   Milestones: _____ Target Date _____ Status _____
   Baseline Fluency Assessment
   Daily Reading Practice Begins

7. **Reflection at the end of the contract:**
   • What improvements have I noticed in my reading fluency?
   • What strategies helped me the most?
   • What challenges did I face, and how did I overcome them?
   • How will I continue to build my fluency in the future?

8. **Signatures:**
   Learner's Signature: _____ Date: _____
   Mentor/Instructor's Signature: _____ Date: _____

Write Social Stories

Initially developed by Gray (2015), social stories are short, personalized narratives designed to teach individuals with autism appropriate social behaviors and responses in specific situations. They provide extra help for students beyond universal classroom strategies, especially when paired with teacher modeling and role-playing. By using social stories consistently, students develop a clearer understanding of social norms, thereby reducing anxiety and behavioral issues. They should be intensive and individualized for students with significant learning or behavioral needs, and they allow students to mentally rehearse social situations and behaviors in a safe, structured way.

For a student struggling with lunchtime routines, for example, a social story could outline each step: waiting in line, engaging in polite conversation, and cleaning up. By repeating these scenarios, the student becomes more familiar with how to act and what to expect. Over time, the anxiety of the situation fades, and the student can navigate the social setting with greater ease and confidence, thanks to the preparation and practice provided by social stories.

Another variation on this strategy is picture strips or visual schedules to support students with multiple exceptionalities, especially students on the autism spectrum. They help reinforce routines, teach social expectations, and improve communication using simple, clear language and visuals. Picture strips use sequences of images to break down tasks, routines, or communication into manageable steps. Figure 4.6 shows a simple yet powerful visual schedule—a foundational support for very young learners and for students with limited expressive language. Though its design may seem basic, this kind of visual aid often marks a turning point in classrooms serving high-needs learners.

By providing clear, predictable visual cues, a schedule such as this helps students anticipate what comes next, reducing anxiety and increasing their ability to transition smoothly between tasks. When consistently used, it strengthens both social and academic participation, giving students a concrete framework to understand routines and expectations. For many classrooms, establishing such a visual schedule is not merely helpful but the essential first step toward building communication, confidence, and independence. Display them on desks or walls, attach them to a lanyard, or use Velcro strips to make them interactive. Don't forget to anticipate the transitions and what is coming next, and always point to the image!

Figure 4.6 Example of a Visual Schedule

| classroom | reading | preferred activity | writing |

Use Speech-to-Text Tools

Speech-to-text technology can be a game-changer for students who struggle with writing. Tools such as Dragon NaturallySpeaking, Microsoft Office, and Google Docs allow students to express their thoughts through dictation, and these tools quickly turn their words into text. Judith worked with a special education teacher who had a student who found writing challenging because his thoughts often raced faster than his hand could keep up. After trying a few different strategies, the special education team decided to give a speech-to-text tool a shot. At first, the student was hesitant, but once he gave it a try, he was hooked. He spoke his ideas, and the tool transcribed them instantly. From that point on, he was able to express his thoughts more freely—whether for essays, reports, or even emails. Over time, his confidence grew as he realized he could communicate more efficiently and share his voice through writing. Technology tools that convert spoken words into written text can be transformative in the general education classroom for students who struggle with writing, whether they possess an individualized education program (IEP) or not.

Integrate IEP Goals

Though it is legally required that students with IEPs have specific goals tailored to their learning needs, the true impact of these goals is realized when teachers intentionally integrate them into everyday classroom instruction. By incorporating IEP goals into general education classroom activities, teachers not only meet legal obligations but also make learning more attainable for students with disabilities. When these goals are taught in the general education classroom, rather than in isolation or separate resource settings, all students benefit. Strategies such as visual supports, hands-on activities, and graphic organizers, which are often used for students with an IEP, enhance learning for everyone, raising the quality of instruction.

For example, in one high school English class, a student with a reading comprehension goal received targeted support during group reading activities. The teacher used graphic organizers, specific reading strategies, and personalized questions aligned with the student's IEP, ensuring that the student could participate fully while receiving the support they needed. Similarly, for students with social interaction goals, teachers might set up peer collaborations or teamwork activities. These integrated approaches not only support students with IEPs but often benefit their peers as well.

Vaughn and colleagues (2014) emphasize that students with disabilities are most successful when general and special educators collaborate to integrate IEP goals and related supports into everyday instruction. They note that strategies such as differentiated instruction, visual supports, and graphic organizers benefit all learners in inclusive classrooms.

This chapter reaffirms that inclusive teaching is not about lowering expectations; it's about widening access so every learner can succeed. By using explicit instruction, flexible pacing, visual supports, and differentiated strategies, general education teachers can ensure that students with special needs and multilingual learners are fully engaged participants in classroom learning. The strategies outlined emphasize that with thoughtful planning, collaborative structures, and intentional scaffolding, all students can meet rigorous standards while developing confidence and independence. Ultimately, inclusive classrooms thrive when teachers see diversity as a source of strength and design lessons that make success achievable for everyone.

5

Technology Integration

Teachers face the ongoing challenge of effectively blending digital resources with traditional methods, and this chapter is all about these challenges. Here, balance is key. The trick is finding the sweet spot between tech and traditional teaching strategies. Students glued to screens all day is a surefire recipe for burnout, but cutting technology out completely could leave them unprepared for the digital world in which they live (Gabriel et al., 2022). John Hattie (2023) captures this dilemma well; he points out that thoughtful use of technology can really boost learning, yet he cautions against pitfalls such as letting smartphones take over the classroom. Successfully managing this balance requires thoughtful strategies, clear guidelines, attention to student well-being, and, above all, a firm grounding in evidence-based instructional practices. Technology should always serve high-quality teaching and learning. In short, it must enhance instruction, never overshadow it.

Blending innovation with intention, this chapter shares more than 70 digital-era strategies to balance screens with strong teaching and elevate student engagement. Strategies in this chapter are sorted into three tiers to indicate how much effort and preparation are involved:

- Immediate, Low-Prep Strategies
- Routine, Moderate-Prep Strategies
- Long-Term, High-Prep Strategies

Immediate, Low-Prep Strategies

Use Technology as a Spice

Consider thinking of technology as a pinch of seasoning that enhances the lesson; it's an ingredient rather than an entire meal. In other words, use tech deliberately where it adds flavor. Research backs this balanced approach. A global education report found that student performance actually drops when classroom tech use goes beyond a moderate amount (UNESCO, 2023). In practice, when devices dominate every activity, kids may sit silently staring at screens instead of interacting with one another. One practical remedy to this is to mix in short tech activities (like a quick Kahoot quiz, a virtual field trip segment, or a paired-shared writing activity on a Google Doc) during a class discussion or hands-on lab work. Treating digital tools like spices—used in just the right spots and amounts—helps ensure that the lesson's core (the main dish) still shines, with technology amplifying the learning instead of overpowering it.

Embrace the Glitch

It always happens: the Wi-Fi inevitably cuts out right as the teacher is about to play a clip, or the brand-new app freezes when the class is deep into a lesson. Rather than times of frustration, these moments can be turned into minilessons on patience and problem solving, both for students and for the teacher. Have a backup plan (veteran teachers often keep a quick offline game ready), but also model a flexible mindset when tech fails. A North Carolina principal told his staff he wanted them to take risks with new tech and that if a lesson flopped, "Don't worry about it"; just learn from it and try again (Will, 2019).

This kind of fail-forward attitude creates a classroom culture where it's OK if the smartboard goes haywire. The teacher might laugh it off and say, "Well, that didn't work. Time for Plan B!" In fact, sharing minor tech fails and recovery strategies transparently with the class models a flexible mindset for students. When students notice their teachers handling tech mishaps with a laugh or shrug instead of stress, they start picking up on that same attitude. They realize glitches are just part of the tech experience. Therefore, the next time an app decides to freeze? Pause, smile, and maybe even invite students to help figure it out. After all, each glitch is just another chance to teach problem solving in action. By showing that a tech failure isn't the end of the world, teachers encourage students to be bold and innovative—with the understanding that mistakes are just steps in the learning process.

Ride Digital Tandem Bikes

Have you ever watched two people riding a tandem bike? To keep moving smoothly, they have to talk and pedal together. Try capturing that same energy in the classroom by having students pair up or form small groups to share devices or tackle projects together. Sure, it might seem odd now that everyone's chasing a 1:1 device ratio, but sometimes teamwork offers more learning power than simply having more tech.

Wang and Le (2022) discovered that in some scenarios, groups of 5th graders sharing one tablet outperformed those who each worked on their own device. The reason? When students team up, they talk more, think aloud, and keep one another on track instead of getting lost in solo screen time. For example, instead of each student doing an individual online research task, the teacher assigns teams of two or three to one computer to brainstorm and fact-find together. During a coding activity, a teacher might designate one student as the "driver" (who writes the code and controls the keyboard) and another as the "navigator" (who checks the code and keeps the big picture in mind). Then they swap roles—a spin on paired programming. This approach turns technology into a social catalyst. What might have been a boring research task becomes a chance for students to team up, and an individual laptop becomes a collaborative hub. The technology hasn't gone anywhere, but instead of keeping students apart, it's now bringing them together.

Embrace Digital Civility

The digital world can be tricky. The information provided—or even the app selected—might be a Trojan horse carrying *unsuspected treasures*. What may seem like a simple game, video platform, or social app can also open doors to unexpected opportunities for learning, creativity, and connection when used intentionally. For instance, a photo-sharing app can become a tool for visual storytelling or science documentation, while a video platform can host authentic student presentations, collaborative projects, or peer feedback sessions. The key is teaching students—and their families—how to uncover the "treasures" while avoiding the traps.

Educators play a vital role in modeling digital curiosity balanced with caution. Consider guiding families and students toward reputable sites and apps that promote responsible engagement and digital literacy. For example, the site Common Sense Media (2024) offers detailed reviews, lesson plans, and toolkits that help teachers and parents understand the benefits and risks of various online tools. Encouraging families to explore these vetted resources together reinforces digital civility as a shared responsibility. When schools and families partner in this way, students learn not only how to protect themselves online but also how to use digital platforms thoughtfully—to learn, create, and connect with integrity.

Routine, Moderate-Prep Strategies

Perform Tech Trust Falls

Handing over some tech responsibility can empower students and lighten the load. Just like a trust fall in team-building exercises, sometimes teachers have to lean back and let the students catch them—or, in this case, let them lead with technology. For instance, the teacher could appoint a few "student tech gurus" in each class to troubleshoot basic issues or help peers on projects.

At an elementary school in Wisconsin, teachers created a student tech team. They found that it provided "effective student assistance for younger learners" and even became a "wonderful support system" for the whole school's tech integration (Busch, 2016, para. 4). There's research to back this up. In an Australian study, teachers who partnered with student "digital leaders" felt more supported and were more willing to try new tech tools (Jackson, 2022). The primary takeaway is that trusting students with meaningful tech roles—whether managing the class blog, being a Zoom cohost, or helping design an interactive quiz—builds their skills and creates a shared ownership of the classroom's digital work. The teacher is no longer the only driver of the tech bus; they've got a handful of copilots.

Tamarra saw this strategy come to life in her school when a student was designated as the tech assistant for the administrative team. Much like the "student tech gurus" and "digital leaders" described earlier, this student played a key role in supporting others—setting up technology for assemblies, meetings, and parent events and assisting with applications that were new to staff. Initially unsure about interacting with adults, the student grew in both technical expertise and confidence. Over time, he mastered tech tasks and began offering ideas and insights to school leaders, becoming a true partner in the school's operations. This example reinforces how handing over meaningful tech responsibilities can elevate student voice, develop leadership skills, and build a culture of shared digital ownership beyond the classroom.

Implement Screen-Free Days

We all know it can be tough to get the balance right between tech and traditional activities in the classroom. It's kind of like putting together a good meal—you want a little bit of everything. Students benefit most when there's a healthy mix of digital learning and hands-on experiences. To help with this, some teachers are now giving tech-free days a shot, dedicating one day a week to shutting down screens entirely. These days let students get back to some basics: pencil-and-paper activities, hands-on group projects, or meaningful face-to-face discussions. The good news? Early studies are beginning to back this approach as beneficial.

One study with middle school students implemented a "digital detox" and found a clear reduction in screen dependency; initially, 20 percent of students showed high levels of screen dependency, which dropped to 14 percent after the intervention, with many other students moving from moderate to lower dependency levels (Abdallah & Ali, 2023). Mental health studies noted similar findings. A 2022 Digital Wellness Lab survey found direct associations between youth media use and perceptions of their emotional and social well-being.

One secondary English teacher, who had extensively integrated technology into her lessons, began implementing "Tech-Free Tuesdays," during which students switched off all devices and completed their reading, writing, and research entirely with paper materials. Though initially resistant, students gradually became more engaged during small-group discussions and collaborative activities, and the teacher observed positive carryover effects into the rest of the weekly activities. This intentional approach to moderating technology aligns with the research highlighting both the cognitive and emotional benefits of periodic breaks from screens (Abdallah & Ali, 2023). In addition, tech-free tasks may improve academic performance; Flanigan and colleagues (2024) conducted a meta-analysis and found that students perform better on assessments when they take notes by hand rather than on a keyboard.

Jump into the Digital Sandbox

Set up "digital sandbox" time for students to play and tinker with new tools without fear of messing up. Just as kids explore freely in a sandbox, students need a low-stakes space to discover what technology can do. The play-based learning advocate and MIT professor Mitchel Resnick (2018) advocated that computers should be seen more like paintbrushes and less like televisions and used as tools for interactive work. What does that look like in practice? The teacher might introduce a new app or device by giving the class 15 minutes of pure exploration time—no grades, no objectives. For example, if the class is starting a unit with a video-editing app, let students film something silly and discover features on their own. You might find they often learn tricks you hadn't thought of! This sandbox approach, supported by play-based learning research, turns initial curiosity into a driving force for learning. Students feel ownership and confidence with the tech because they have uncovered how it works.

Foster Digital Student Engagement

Monica Burns (2023, 2024) advocates for various digital strategies to enhance student engagement by leveraging technology in purposeful and interactive ways:

- Use digital portfolios, where students can organize and showcase their work over time. This tactic makes student reflection and ownership of learning easier to ascertain.
- Bringing in gamified elements such as digital badges or fun, challenge-based activities can really fire up student motivation. Students naturally enjoy a bit of friendly competition, so these strategies often lead to higher engagement and enthusiasm in class.
- Use AR and VR in class because this technology lets students dive into realistic simulations or virtual tours. Students get

genuinely excited when abstract topics suddenly become tangible and easy to grasp.

- Encourage students to get involved in podcasting projects. They research topics they're interested in, write scripts, and record their own episodes, which boosts their speaking confidence and media awareness.
- Have students create their own digital projects—such as presentations or digital storytelling. Crafting content helps them sharpen communication and digital literacy skills.
- To keep tabs on student learning, use interactive methods such as live polls or digital exit slips, which provide an instant insight into how students are doing and what they might need next.
- Utilize digital choice boards and let students pick from different activities. Being able to work in ways students prefer really helps them take charge of their learning and stay motivated.
- Use AI-powered apps and tools designed specifically to adapt lessons for different student needs. Ultimately, technology should make learning more meaningful—not replace the interactions and engagement students thrive on.

These strategies, drawn from Burns's books and website, illustrate how thoughtful technology integration can boost student engagement during lessons while balancing digital and traditional learning experiences.

Teachers often rush to type the first question that comes to mind when using AI tools for lesson planning or feedback. *The Step-Back AI Prompt Planner,* adapted from Google's prompt engineering guide, reframes that habit (Boonstra, 2025). It trains teachers to pause and craft one high-quality prompt that clarifies *purpose, context,* and *constraints*—just as they would when designing an effective learning task.

Step 1: Define the purpose. Before writing the prompt, name exactly what the model is expected to produce.

- Start with a verb of intent: *summarize, generate, classify, rewrite, design, scaffold.*
- Add the learner outcome needed: "to support 5th grade vocabulary development," "to model a standards-based rubric."
- Examples: "Generate a three-part writing prompt to strengthen 6th grade argument writing." "Design a 15-minute developmentally appropriate lesson plan for 3- or 4-year-olds about expressing feelings."

Step 2: Add context. AI models respond best when given background, tone, and limits.

- Include who the audience is and what they already know.
- Name the format and scope: number of paragraphs, tone, reading level, or resource limits.
- Examples: "Act as a middle school literacy coach helping new teachers design a 15-minute station activity." "Act as a first-time preschool teacher and generate outdoor learning stations around the theme of balls."

Step 3: Step back and refine. Before pressing "enter," take a step back. Self-reflect on the meta-prompt: "What broader question or general principle would make this prompt stronger or more accurate?" This reflective step—borrowed directly from step-back prompting—activates critical reasoning and reveals missing conditions. Consider revising the earlier example to "List three ways to differentiate this 15-minute station for multilingual learners before creating the final version."

Step 4: Keep for future use. Consider keeping your generated prompts for future use. This can allow you to share with others, review the prompts for improvement, and create a bank of effective prompts for multiple uses.

Clarity precedes creativity. When purpose and constraints are explicit, AI output improves. The disciplined pause before generating a prompt mirrors the metacognitive reflection teachers model for students, reinforcing awareness of process over impulse. Over time, this structured cycle of defining purpose, contextualizing need, and reflecting on outcome becomes a transferable habit for designing questions, lessons, and feedback. Each intentional pause between typing and sending becomes an act of professional development, sharpening both precision and pedagogical insight.

Long-Term, High-Prep Strategies

Develop Teacher Training and Support

Technology integration in education is a movement, but there's no one-size-fits-all approach. Different countries and districts have developed unique strategies to help teachers manage and use technology effectively in K–12 classrooms. In high-performing education systems, a common theme is strong teacher training and support for using digital tools. Modern education systems recognize that as technology evolves, teachers need continuous professional development to keep up (Gabriel et al., 2022; Raave et al., 2024).

For example, Portugal launched a nationwide digital program for schools focusing on teacher communities of practice and peer learning, ensuring educators learn with and from one another as they adopt tech (Gabriel et al., 2022). Ireland recently adopted UNESCO's ICT Competency Framework into its teacher training courses. When researchers reviewed the impact, they discovered it made a big difference—teachers felt much more comfortable and motivated to bring digital tools into their classrooms (Gabriel et al., 2022). In Germany, a national "Education in the Digital World" plan made teacher digital literacy an essential requirement, prompting extensive training so teachers can use tech pedagogically soundly (UNESCO, 2023). In the United States, influential edtech author Monica Burns advocates collaborating with educators beyond their immediate environment by using videoconferencing tools and enriching teaching practices through diverse perspectives (Burns, 2023).

Whether through formal courses, peer mentoring, or online teacher communities, investing in their ability to manage classroom technology effectively places teachers on par with educators worldwide. Consider investing in innovative teaching strategies, professional development, technology integration resources, and supportive colleagues focused on enhancing student learning through technology.

Encourage Student-Led Digital Citizenship

Keith worked with a middle school social studies teacher in Texas who noticed increased online conflicts and inappropriate use of technology after his school district distributed notebooks to every student. Determined to address these challenges proactively, the teacher decided to initiate a student-driven campaign promoting responsible digital behavior. His students eagerly brainstormed and adopted the slogan "Think Twice, Click Once" and created engaging TikTok-style videos showcasing positive and negative examples of online interactions. Counselors noticed improvements almost immediately, reporting far fewer cases of online bullying. Even better, students naturally picked up on the campaign's messaging, casually encouraging one another to stay respectful and careful online. This example aligns with research indicating that empowering students to lead digital literacy initiatives can significantly improve online behavior (Digital Wellness Lab, 2024).

Manage a Flipped Classroom

A middle school math teacher in California recently noticed a big jump in her students' involvement after switching to a flipped classroom. After she began assigning short, interactive video lessons for homework, class time opened up for meaningful discussions, group problem solving, and practical activities. She soon noticed students naturally contributing more to conversations and jumping into writing tasks more confidently. She was clear that explicit instruction still made up around 20–40 percent of her lessons, but flipping her classroom allowed her to spend more class time on group projects and active learning. She credited these improvements directly to flipping the way she taught. This matches what recent research has found: that flipping the classroom can help students grasp concepts better and remember information longer compared to typical lecture methods (Raave et al., 2024).

Thoughtfully Incorporate Artificial Intelligence

With AI quickly becoming a regular part of education, teachers are working hard to help students use it thoughtfully while still taking advantage of its classroom benefits. Many educators now include lessons specifically on AI literacy, showing students how to spot biases, question AI-generated materials, and double-check the accuracy of what they find. Some schools have implemented AI use policies, guiding students on ethical AI applications such as using chatbots for brainstorming but not for plagiarism. One middle school teacher we've observed encourages students to compare AI-generated responses with their own writing to develop critical thinking and originality.

Meanwhile, other teachers are using AI-powered tools for grading, feedback, and lesson customization—adapting the readability of texts, generating practice and quiz questions (e.g., Gradescope, Writable, ChatGPT, Copilot), and performing data analysis (e.g., Freckle,

Lexia Core5, i-Ready) but with human oversight to ensure fairness and accuracy (Burns, 2024). Plenty of teacher resources are available online (e.g., Scratch Foundation, 2024) to help integrate AI into play-based learning. AI can be a powerful classroom tool when used with structured guidance and ethical considerations (Raave et al., 2024).

Ultimately, effective technology integration is about balance and intentionality. When digital tools are used purposefully—not as distractions or replacements for strong teaching—they amplify engagement, creativity, and connection in the classroom. Whether through student-led projects, screen-free days, or ethical use of AI, teachers can model how to use technology with curiosity, care, and discernment. The heart of great instruction remains human: clear goals, authentic relationships, and meaningful learning experiences. When educators blend these timeless principles with thoughtful tech practices, they prepare students not only to succeed in school but also to thrive as responsible, adaptable learners in an ever-evolving digital world.

6

Family Involvement

Teachers often encounter a broad spectrum of family involvement, from overly hands-on parents to completely disengaged ones. This chapter provides more than 50 of the latest actionable, innovative strategies to help educators foster positive relationships with families and create meaningful engagement opportunities that support student learning. The strategies presented in this chapter are classified by how much planning and effort they require, organized into three clear categories:

- Immediate, Low-Prep Strategies
- Routine, Moderate-Prep Strategies
- Long-Term, High-Prep Strategies

Immediate, Low-Prep Strategies

Create Interactive Newsletters

Some tech-savvy teachers are giving the old classroom newsletter a fresh spin and turning it into an interactive tool that strengthens connections with families. Instead of long, text-heavy updates, these newsletters include colorful visuals, easy-to-read translations, short videos from the teacher, student work samples, and formats that are simple to view on a phone. Whether the teacher issues a newsletter weekly, monthly, or with every new unit, they should work to make the format interactive.

Many teachers embed Google Forms polls to let parents vote on topics such as field trip destinations or which novel unit to address. This tactic ensures families maintain a direct voice in shaping class experiences. Others create short quizzes related to current studies—perhaps a science unit—and invite parents and children to complete them together; this reinforces in-class learning at home and encourages families to actively engage with content in ways that fit into their schedules and preferences. This tactic promotes the notion of parents as active participants (Epstein et al., 2018; Epstein & Sheldon, 2023).

Some teachers take it a step further by adding simple, curriculum-based "family challenges" to their newsletters. After a lesson on historical figures, for example, adults at home might be invited to create a short video or drawing together and send it in to share with the class. These simple shifts turn newsletters from basic updates to interactive tools that welcome families into the learning process. Instead of just sharing information, they help create meaningful connections between school and home, building a sense of teamwork and shared purpose that carries learning beyond the classroom.

Use Strategies for Managing Challenging Parent Behaviors

Even the most dedicated educators encounter difficult moments with parents—those tense conversations when emotions run high, communication breaks down, or good intentions get lost in frustration. The key is to approach these interactions with empathy, composure, and a partnership mindset (Epstein & Sheldon, 2023). When teachers intentionally deescalate conflict and refocus discussions on shared goals, they preserve trust and strengthen the home–school connection. The following strategies provide practical ways to turn challenging conversations into productive collaboration (Young et al., 2023):

- **Recognize positive intent.** Acknowledging that parents usually have their child's best interests at heart can help deescalate tension. For example, suppose a parent questions teaching methods. In that case, the teacher might respond, "I appreciate how invested you are in [student's name]'s learning experience, and I completely understand you're looking out for their best interests. I'm committed to helping your child, too, so let's take a closer look at how my approach works and discuss any adjustments we might consider." Alternatively, for a defensive parent, say, "I understand why this situation might be upsetting. I can tell how deeply you care about [student's name]'s well-being and progress. I'm here to support your child, just like you. Can we discuss ways to partner more effectively together to help them succeed?"

- **Ask for or offer help.** Inviting parents to share what they need or suggesting ways the teacher can support them fosters collaboration and demonstrates respect for their perspectives. If a parent repeatedly becomes frustrated or confused with classroom policies or assignments and expresses irritation, the teacher might say, "I understand why this feels frustrating. Could you tell me more about what support might be most helpful to you right now? I'd really like to assist however I can. Could I clarify something specific, or would it help if we reviewed assignments together briefly each week?"

- **Honor expertise or experience.** Valuing parents' knowledge of their children builds trust and encourages a more balanced conversation. For a parent who is skeptical of the teacher's assessment of their child's behavior or performance, insisting that the child never struggles at home, a response might be "I truly value your insight because nobody knows your child better than you. You have a unique experience with [student's name] at home. I'd appreciate hearing more about the strategies that work well for you so we can find common ground and support your child effectively here at school."

- **Reflect and redirect.** Fully acknowledging and summarizing the parent's concerns (reflect) and guiding the conversation toward constructive options (redirect) keeps communication productive. For a parent who expresses frustration at the teacher, claiming they aren't doing enough to support their child academically, the teacher might reflect, saying, "I hear that you're feeling disappointed and frustrated because you believe we could be doing more for [student's name] academically." Then redirect: "Let's look at specific ways to increase support. Would it help to set up regular check-ins to discuss progress and look at other strategies or resources?"

- **Say, "thanks..."** Expressing gratitude for the parent's input, even when critical, helps maintain positive rapport and shows that their concerns are taken seriously. With a parent who emails frequently with highly critical feedback, questioning every classroom decision, perhaps the teacher can reply with "Thank you for telling me your concerns and perspectives. This helps me reflect and grow. I appreciate your investment in [student's name]'s school experience. Let's find a time to discuss these concerns in person and ensure we're on the same sheet of music moving forward."

- **Apologize.** When appropriate, it is important to offer a sincere apology. Acknowledging missteps and committing to improvement demonstrate humility and respect. When a parent is upset due to a genuine mistake, such as miscommunication about a deadline or losing a student's assignment, say, "You're right. I made a mistake, and I sincerely apologize. I recognize that this caused frustration for both you and [student's name], and that's not acceptable. Please know I've already adjusted my process to ensure it doesn't happen again. Can we discuss the next steps to ensure [student's name] feels supported moving forward?"

Leverage Social Data

Modern teachers leverage various platforms and formats to demonstrate the positive impact of their instructional strategies transparently without compromising student privacy. Rather than relying solely on end-of-term reports, teachers frequently share social data—informal yet meaningful evidence of student growth—in the form of anonymous anecdotes, snapshots of classwide improvement, or general testimonials, often supported by pictures, brief video clips, or samples of student work. For instance, a teacher might send out a digital newsletter highlighting how a student mastered new phonics skills, accompanied by a short audio clip of a child's reading. This approach aligns with the ongoing emphasis in partnership research on communicating student progress clearly and positively between home and school (Epstein et al., 2018).

Crucially, in these instances, teachers always anonymize or secure permission for individual student information, ensuring that privacy remains paramount. Alternatively, secure classroom platforms (such as ClassDojo or Seesaw) allow teachers to post real-time updates celebrating collective milestones, such as successful science experiments or group projects fostering teamwork and friendships, without identifying individual students by name.

This approach goes beyond merely sharing "good news" stories; it also sheds light on the instructional methods that underpin these successes. Teachers regularly annotate these examples with brief explanations of specific strategies, such as a new peer-tutoring method or recent reading stations, and highlight why and how these approaches generally benefit the class or individual learners without singling out specific student deficits or successes. By transparently connecting each achievement to intentional teaching practices, parents gain valuable insights into how classroom methods support academic and social-emotional growth for all students. This consistent yet privacy-conscious communication fosters trust and demonstrates teachers' dedication to helping every child thrive. In addition, social data provides valuable context for understanding the how and why behind formal assessment results, further enhancing the school–home partnership.

Build Parent–Teacher Alliances

Building strong, productive alliances with parents requires genuine interest, consistent attention, and a clear vision of the partnership. Even if a teacher is more reserved by nature, they can approach each interaction with parents as an opportunity to discover something new about them, their backgrounds, or what motivates their children's learning (Epstein et al., 2018). Remembering a small detail about their family or child's interests makes follow-up conversations more meaningful. Although trust and rapport are essential, try not to confuse partnership with friendship. Consider other respected professionals, such as family doctors or mechanics, who earn clients' confidence without crossing personal boundaries. Reflect on what actions fit into this kind of trusted, respectful alliance, and use that image to guide decisions.

The teacher needs to maintain a focus on supporting the student's academic and personal growth, sharing just enough personal experience, philosophy, and relevant background to establish credibility and empathy. Disclosing stories about professional achievements or insights on educational strategies can inspire parents, but the teacher should think twice before oversharing personal struggles or opinions unrelated to their child's progress. Conversations need to be centered on helping the student thrive by demonstrating a helpful learning technique, listening to parents' concerns, or clarifying classroom goals. By striking this balance, teachers build collaborative environments where parents feel respected, informed, and motivated to support their child's education—without blurring the lines of professionalism.

Develop Targeted Parent Support

When communicating with parents about their student's progress, consider the following tips:

- **Speak from data.** Sharing objective data helps keep conversations focused and clear, reducing the likelihood of personal biases influencing the discussion, positively or negatively. Address questions such as *What are the student's scores? In what areas has the student shown strength? How was this strength observed? What specific goals has the student set for improvement?*

- **Speak with the intent to improve student learning.** Conversations with parents should remain constructive, emphasizing solutions rather than frustrations about what a student has or hasn't done. Focus clearly on actionable steps: "Considering Giovanni's recent writing scores, here are two steps we'll take to enhance his writing. First, he'll read his writing aloud to identify missing words. If possible, encourage him to read aloud to you as well. Second, Giovanni will review each sentence for correct capitalization and punctuation. I've provided some example sentences he can use as models." This approach offers hope, clarity, and direction.

- **Discuss support strategies rather than focusing solely on problems.** For example, say, "Giovanni loves to draw. You might encourage him to illustrate his next story and then describe the drawing to you. We'll also use this strategy in class." Being explicit about how parents can academically support their child helps them see how they can actively participate.

- **Speak with positive presupposition.** Demonstrating appreciation and collaboration sets a positive tone. Say, "Thank you for taking the time to discuss Giovanni's progress. I know he is eager to succeed. Do you have other ideas or insights about how I might better support his learning? When you review his writing or drawings, I would greatly value your feedback." Assuming parents have their child's best interests at heart and can contribute meaningful strategies helps build a genuine partnership in supporting the child's learning.

- **Speak clearly and respectfully without educational jargon.** Explaining teaching methods and educational concepts in clear, everyday language builds relationships. Parents often feel alienated or unintentionally disrespected when teachers use technical or academic jargon excessively. Communicating clearly without specialized terminology helps parents feel respected, engaged, and confident in their ability to collaborate effectively in their child's education.

Routine, Moderate-Prep Strategies

Hold Difficult Conversations

Before tackling a sensitive topic with a parent or caregiver, it's worth putting real thought into how the teacher will approach it. Maybe a student has been pulling back during class discussions, or perhaps a belief held at home is quietly affecting how that child engages with learning. These conversations can be tough, but with a bit of thoughtful preparation, you can approach them with clarity, empathy, and a problem-solving mindset. The aim isn't to place blame; it's to build trust and create a path forward that truly supports the student's growth (Epstein et al., 2018).

One teacher with whom we worked needed to engage a father who kept telling his daughter that the entire family struggled with math and that she would probably struggle as well. This formed a parental expectation detrimental to the student's academic success. Preparing ahead of time can help the teacher approach the conversation with clarity, empathy, and confidence. The following steps— pulled from the work of Aguilar (2024), Anderson and Buchko

(2016), and Young and colleagues (2023)—can help the teacher feel more prepared and steady going into a tough conversation with a parent or caregiver.

- **Clarify the belief or issue.** Write out the exact belief, behavior, or issue you need to address. Getting it down in clear, simple terms can help you stay focused and avoid drifting off track during the conversation. Remember, this part is not necessarily going to be shared with anyone. Use clear, factual data points—such as notes from observations, student work samples, survey results, or assessment data—that illustrate why the conversation is necessary.

- **Consider the parent's perspective.** Based on the information available, the teacher can hypothesize why a parent may hold a particular belief. Reflecting on the possible reasons behind the parent's viewpoint will help the teacher approach the parent with respect and understanding. In fact, it may be possible to find a positive reason for them to hold this belief, practice, or behavior.

- **Identify the conflict.** To avoid quick misconceptions, a teacher can think through what feels off about the parent's viewpoint or response. Is it clashing with personal teaching values or beliefs? Is it holding the student back? Writing this out helps clarify why the issue matters and keeps the conversation focused.

- **Envision reasonable alternatives.** It is important for the teacher to consider what outcome is desired instead of the current belief or behavior. Perhaps sharing research, examples, or concrete strategies with the parent would help. Write these down and think about how to present them clearly and supportively; sometimes a brief handout or a simple graphic illustrating the problem and solution can speak volumes.

- **Plan who should be involved.** If appropriate, the teacher may consider inviting a supportive colleague, counselor, or another staff member who can help maintain a calm, productive environment. The intention is not to overwhelm the parent but to ensure the conversation is balanced, constructive, and focused on the student's best interests.
- **Anticipate arguments.** Brainstorm potential objections the parent might raise and prepare a thoughtful, empathetic response to each. A well-thought-out plan can keep the conversation on track even when surprises arise.
- **Be open to new information.** The parent may disclose concerns or issues the teacher was not aware of—perhaps related to the family's circumstances, the child's well-being, or the family's religious understanding. While listening and acknowledging these factors, staying committed to addressing the original issue is essential. If this conversation is warranted, the underlying concern remains significant.
- **Acknowledge hopes and fears.** Consider the best possible outcome and the most challenging scenario. Being realistic about potential outcomes helps in maintaining composure, whatever the result.
- **Set clear next steps.** Plan how to ask the parent to consider changing their approach. Agree on what evidence or indicators teacher and parent should revisit, and set a timeline for a follow-up discussion; this practice increases the likelihood that the conversation leads to ongoing, measurable progress.

If, after careful planning, the teacher is still unsure about how to approach the discussion, role-playing with a trusted colleague or mentor might be considered. Practicing the conversation in advance—trying out different ways of phrasing points and responding to potential reactions—often increases confidence and clarity once the meeting with the parent begins.

Solicit Parent Volunteers

Involve parents in supporting classroom activities. Building on Joyce Epstein's framework for family engagement, many teachers find creative and flexible ways for parents to contribute meaningfully as classroom volunteers—both in person and virtually (Epstein et al., 2018; Epstein & Sheldon, 2023). Beyond the traditional classroom helper role, many educators now invite parents to use their professional expertise or cultural background to enrich the curriculum, creating more authentic and homespun student learning experiences. One of the most successful parental involvement strategies is tutoring (effect size = 0.49; Hattie, 2023).

For example, a parent who works as an engineer might join a weekly STEM workshop to guide small groups of students in designing simple machines. By contrast, another parent might share stories, recipes, or family artifacts that bring a social studies unit to life. We watched one mother bring a schoolhouse bell, a tattered quilt, and letters from her family's experience on the Oregon Trail, all of which supported the westward expansion unit being studied by the class. These contributions sharpen students' understanding of content and help them see connections between what they learn in class and the wider world.

Technology has also opened up new possibilities for parent volunteering. With the rise of online platforms, teachers sometimes host virtual career fairs where parents log in from their workplaces—factories, farms, offices, hospitals—to give short presentations and answer questions about what they do. Others encourage parents to prerecord read-alouds or cultural storytimes that the teacher can integrate into daily lessons, providing students with exposure to diverse languages, dialects, and narratives. Some schools tap tech-savvy parent volunteers to curate age-appropriate online resources or create short tutorial videos, helping students navigate digital research tools. In these ways, parents become valuable co-educators, partnering with teachers to offer a richer and more connected learning environment.

Distribute Parent Feedback Surveys

Collect input from parents to adjust and improve engagement strategies. In the wake of pandemic-related disruptions to learning and behavior, teachers worldwide are reimagining parent feedback surveys as more than just static questionnaires. They're making these surveys more dynamic, accessible, and culturally responsive, using them as starting points for ongoing dialogue. For instance, some educators distribute short, mobile-friendly surveys designed for quick completion during a parent's busy commute or break. Rather than sending out a long form at the end of the semester, teachers issue brief, targeted polls on specific topics, such as new reading routines or recently introduced social-emotional learning activities. Therefore, feedback arrives in time to inform immediate adjustments. This agile approach ensures that parental insights guide mid-course corrections rather than serving as after-the-fact reflections.

Beyond simply collecting data, teachers also use survey results as conversation starters. After sharing summarized, anonymous feedback with families, they hold follow-up online roundtables or brief Q&A sessions to co-create solutions that address identified concerns. Some schools incorporate translation tools and culturally sensitive language into surveys, ensuring inclusivity and encouraging broader participation. Others implement embedded multimedia, such as short videos or examples of student work, to give parents context for the questions they're answering. Teachers are closing the feedback loop by presenting survey results to parents and the steps they plan to take in response. This transparency builds trust, validates parents' voices, and directly connects their input to school improvements, helping tackle academic and behavioral challenges more collaboratively and effectively.

Long-Term, High-Prep Strategies

Hold Family Group Conferences

Regular, structured meetings keep parents informed and trained as co-teachers. Family group conferences are a structured approach to family engagement that enhances student academic outcomes by fostering collaboration between teachers and families (Epstein et al., 2018; Epstein & Sheldon, 2023). This model involves three 60–90-minute group meetings (along with any additional needed individual sessions) throughout the academic year. During the group meetings, all parents convene to review grade-level skills, analyze aggregated and individual student data, and learn specific activities to support their children's learning at home. Think of basic foundation skills from the learning standards, such as letter recognition, reading fluency, and math facts at the lower grades or sentence combining and study skills in the upper grades. These sessions can replace most traditional one-on-one parent–teacher conferences, ensuring no additional time burden on teachers. This structure is informed by the works of Joyce Epstein (Epstein et al., 2018; Epstein & Sheldon, 2023), who writes prolifically about parents as active school partners, and Chrispeels (1996), Paredes (2010), and WestEd (2016a).

In practice, teachers begin each parent group meeting with a warm-up activity to build community. They then present data on class and individual student performance on a foundational skill or process, highlighting areas for improvement. The heartbeat of this strategy is when the teacher demonstrates a targeted practice activity—such as reading comprehension exercises or math problem-solving techniques—that parents can implement at home. Then parents engage in hands-on practice of these activities in small groups during the meeting to build their confidence.

These steps significantly increase the likelihood that parents deploy the strategy at home. To build accountability, families work with the teacher to set 60–90-day academic goals for their child, creating a shared sense of responsibility. The teacher uses short pre- and post-assessments to track progress along the way, making sure that these partnerships lead to real, measurable growth in learning. Student progress on the goals is shared during subsequent meetings, and new skills and practices are introduced at each of the three sessions. For examples of this tactic, check out the YouTube videos from the Flamboyan Foundation (2012).

Here's a basic agenda for a family group conference:

- Warm Welcome and Connection Activities (10–15 min.): Introduce everyone in a friendly, inclusive manner. Encourage a brief interactive activity to build trust.
- Foundational Skills and Progress Review (15–20 min.): Present essential academic targets and highlight trends. Discuss where students are thriving and where support is needed.
- Demonstration of Effective Learning Strategies (15–20 min.): Show families how to apply evidence-based techniques at home. Model engaging activities and tools that reinforce key concepts.
- Hands-On Family Practice (15–20 min.): Allow everyone to try out the activities together. Answer questions and offer guidance on using take-home materials.
- Collaborative Goal Setting (10–15 min.): Work together to outline achievable objectives for student success. Agree on actionable steps to maintain progress over time. One session occurs in early fall, the second in winter, and the third in spring.

Educators seeking a meaningful approach to family engagement will find this type of parent engagement both practical and highly effective. This structured, teacher-led parent tutoring, combined with explicit instruction for parents to maintain high expectations for their children, aligns closely with several parent engagement activities identified by Hattie (2023) as directly influencing student academic achievement. Specifically, these activities include parent expectations (effect size = 0.50), tutoring (effect size = 0.49), and parental programs (effect size = 0.39).

By harnessing a structured approach such as family group conferences, teachers and families can collaborate effectively to boost student outcomes through clear goal setting, practical at-home strategies, and shared accountability—all supported by evidence-based research.

Organize Family Learning Nights

A fresh take on the traditional curriculum night or math night is to turn those events into ongoing, hands-on family learning labs. Instead of just listing the skills students need to learn, teachers kick things off by modeling a specific strategy—such as how to break down a tricky math problem or use a reading move that supports comprehension. After that, families get a chance to try it out themselves, working through examples in small groups with support from the teacher. This kind of setup gives parents a real sense of how the learning works, so when they head home, they feel equipped and confident to support their child.

To take the experience further, each family sets a short-term academic goal—something achievable within the next two months—with clear, manageable steps. Together, parents, students, and teachers decide how progress will be monitored, using simple tools like check-ins or short teacher-led assessments between sessions. At future learning labs, families and teachers look at how things are going, celebrate what's working, review student progress, and dive into a new skill or strategy. This ongoing cycle of modeling, hands-on practice, goal setting, and follow-up builds real momentum.

Over time, these gatherings can grow into a supportive learning community where families build skills, notice real growth in their children, and stay connected to the learning in a lasting way—not just for one night. While similar in spirit to family group conferences, this approach can involve an entire grade level or even the whole school community.

Offer Parent Training on Social and Emotional Needs

Educators are elevating parent training on social and emotional needs from one-off tip sheets to interactive, ongoing learning experiences. This development of SEL programs aligns with research about the impact of social skills programs on student academic success (effect size = 0.40; Hattie, 2023). At the elementary level, for example, some schools partner with child psychologists or counselors to cohost family emotional wellness nights. Parents and caregivers don't just listen during these events; they engage in hands-on activities. They might practice simple breathing exercises or role-play common conflicts, learning to respond calmly to a child's frustration. Afterward, educators share short, kid-friendly yoga and mindfulness videos that parents can use at home. They also invite parents to join online message boards or social networks moderated by counselors, where they can ask questions and swap strategies with other families navigating similar challenges.

Teachers and school leaders are getting creative with hybrid training sessions, incorporating digital resources and in-person workshops at the secondary level. For instance, one high school hosted an online SEL boot camp for parents, releasing a series of short videos and interactive quizzes about talking to students about stress management, digital citizenship, and conflict resolution. Parents completed the modules at their own pace, then attended an in-person forum where teens, teachers, and mental health experts held candid panel discussions about issues such as anxiety, peer pressure, and self-esteem.

Some schools have also introduced reverse mentoring sessions where students guide parents through understanding social media's emotional impact, role-playing digital dilemmas to practice empathetic responses. This emphasis on two-way interaction—where parents learn not only from teachers and experts but also from students themselves—helps ensure that social and emotional training is relevant, collaborative, and truly supportive of adolescents' needs.

Strong partnerships between families and schools are built on trust, communication, and shared responsibility for student success. When educators intentionally invite parents and caregivers into the learning process—through clear communication, structured collaboration, and meaningful feedback—families become true partners in education rather than passive participants. The strategies in this chapter show that effective engagement isn't about more meetings or messages; it's about building relationships grounded in respect and purpose. By creating welcoming, collaborative, and culturally responsive pathways for families to support learning, teachers strengthen not only academic outcomes but also the sense of community that every thriving school depends on.

7

Assessment and Grading

I n recent years, many of the educators with whom we work have been rethinking traditional grading methods in big and small ways. Letter grades often provide a limited snapshot of a student's understanding and sometimes fail to capture the nuances of their learning journey. This is causing a shift toward mastery-based grading, detailed rubric grading, and more reliance on formative assessment. We're seeing students being given multiple opportunities to demonstrate understanding, ensuring they achieve some level of mastery before progressing. These approaches not only foster deeper comprehension but also help students view challenges as opportunities to learn rather than obstacles to the highest grades.

Complementing mastery-based grading is the idea of personalized instruction, which tailors teaching methods and content to individual student needs. For example, in a 3rd grade classroom, teachers might offer various assessments, including interim and benchmark tests, to gauge student progress. Students who do not master a standard on the first attempt receive additional support and opportunities to reassess, using individual mastery trackers to monitor their development. This personalized approach increases the likelihood that each student's unique learning needs are addressed, leading to increased engagement, improved academic performance, and the promotion of essential life skills such as critical thinking and self-regulation.

This chapter provides more than 100 of the best classroom-based assessments we've encountered that more closely reveal student learning. Furthermore, the reader will find the strategies divided into three levels based on their complexity and preparation demands:

- Immediate, Low-Prep Strategies
- Routine, Moderate-Prep Strategies
- Long-Term, High-Prep Strategies

Immediate, Low-Prep Strategies

Highlight the Way

During independent practice, try walking around the classroom with a highlighter or a colorful stamp to mark students' correct answers as they work quietly. This visual feedback gives students instant feedback, letting them know when they're on track, and positively reinforces their effort immediately. Students get excited when they see their work recognized, and it often sparks a healthy dose of friendly competition—encouraging classmates to double-check their answers or rethink their methods.

In a 4th grade class working through multidigit multiplication problems, the teacher casually moved around the room as students concentrated quietly, marking correct solutions with a bright green highlighter. Pretty soon, students began noticing the highlighted answers around them. This visual feedback naturally energized them to revisit their calculations, compare their strategies with peers, and even spark impromptu discussions about how they solved each problem. The classroom buzzed with meaningful conversations, and learning deepened.

Of course, it's essential to consider how to use this approach. Not every student enjoys having attention drawn to their work—especially those who struggle or feel anxious about public praise. For these students, consider marking their answers more discreetly or using quiet words of encouragement instead of noticeable highlighting. The teacher might pair subtle, supportive feedback with gentle hints or quick one-on-one conversations to help students who seem hesitant or unsure. The key is to stay tuned to each student's comfort level, ensuring your feedback builds confidence rather than stress.

In this way, formative assessment through highlighting correct responses acts like placing flags on a trail: it signals to students that they're headed in the right direction, motivates them to push forward, and guides teachers to those who might need extra support before continuing on their learning journey.

Eliminate SOBOs (Shout-Outs and Blurt-Outs)

It's easy to fall into the habit of accepting shouted-out answers—what we call SOBOs (shout-outs and blurt-outs). They're quick, they make the classroom feel lively, and they give the illusion of broad participation. In reality, though, SOBOs reflect an imbalance of voices. A small number of students dominate the discussion while many others—often quieter students, English learners, or those who process information more slowly—are left unseen and unheard.

Figure 7.1 captures this imbalance visually. The tall, dark lines represent the same few students who consistently call out answers, rising far above their peers. The shorter lines beneath them represent the many students who remain silent—either because they can't compete with the pace of the blurters or because the classroom structure unintentionally signals that only the fastest voices count. When teachers "accept" SOBOs, they unknowingly reinforce inequity, rewarding speed and confidence over reflection and inclusion. This visual helps teachers *see* what is often invisible in real time: the disproportionate participation pattern that emerges when only a few voices dominate. Recognizing this pattern is the first step toward changing it. Replacing SOBOs with equitable engagement routines—such as think-pair-share, everyone writes, or response cards—gives all students structured time to process, contribute, and be heard.

By shifting away from SOBOs, teachers send a powerful message: *every student's thinking matters*. The goal isn't to silence enthusiasm—it's to channel it into a structure that invites everyone into the learning conversation.

Figure 7.1   The Problem of Shout-Outs and Blurt-Outs (SOBOs)

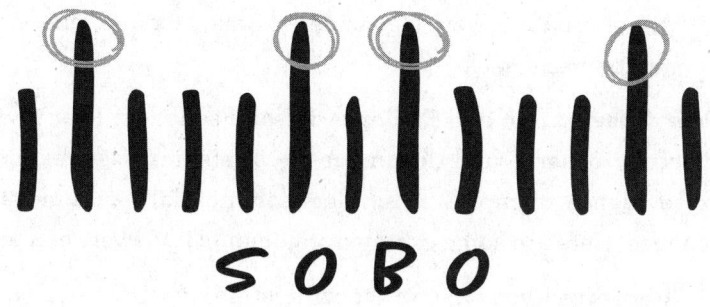

Source: From *The Instructional Coaching Handbook* (p. 93), by A. K. Young, A. B. Julien, and T. Osborne, 2023, ASCD.

Incorporate Peer Review Activities

Incorporate peer evaluations as part of the assessment process and as a key component of the learning and reflection process (distinctly separate from peer grading). Peer review is most effective when clear protocols guide structured conversations, promoting explicit discussion around multiple approaches to solving mathematical problems. Visible learning strategies include peer feedback as highly correlated to student achievement (effect size = 0.50; Hattie, 2024). Through these conversations, students learn from diverse perspectives, actively argue for their own methods, and thoughtfully defend their reasoning.

Structured Protocol for Arguing and Defending Mathematical Thinking: Identify the mathematical skill or concept. Begin by clearly stating, "Today, we are focusing on solving problems involving [specific concept or skill]."

Presentation of Multiple Approaches: Each student explicitly explains their own approach to solving the given problem, clearly articulating each step taken. Here are a few example sentence starters you can provide:

- "My approach to solving this problem was…."
- "First, I decided to… because…."
- "An alternative way I considered was…, but I chose this method because…."

Peer Observation and Evidence-Based Feedback: Peer reviewers carefully observe and document the strategies used, explicitly noting evidence of practical problem-solving skills or innovative approaches. Here are some example statements reviewers can use:

- "I observed your use of [specific strategy]. Specifically, you [describe clearly and explicitly]. What made you choose this particular method?"
- "One clear strength of your approach is… because…."
- "I noticed you chose not to use [alternative approach]. Could you explain why?"

Explicit Argumentation and Defense: Students engage directly by questioning and defending their chosen methods. They articulate the advantages and potential drawbacks of different approaches. Here are some example sentence starters for arguing and defending:

- "I chose this method because [clear explanation rooted in mathematical reasoning]."
- "An advantage of my approach is… compared to your method, which…."
- "I see your point about…, but here's why my approach could be more effective in this scenario…."

Collaborative Reflection and Final Edits: Both participants collaboratively discuss how the reviewed strategies could be improved and refined. Here are a couple of guiding questions for discussion:

- "What new insights did you gain from discussing our different methods?"
- "How might your strategy change after considering other approaches?"

Learning Consolidation: After the discussion, the student makes focused final edits to their original solution or explanation. Conclude each session by asking students to articulate their learning explicitly:

- "What is one significant insight you gained from reviewing your peer's approach?"
- "How will you incorporate today's lessons into future problem-solving situations?"

Using structured conversations and explicit questioning, these peer review activities empower students to confidently argue for their own approaches, thoughtfully consider alternatives, and defend their mathematical thinking.

Routine, Moderate-Prep Strategies

Clarify Objectives

Clearly define assessment criteria and expectations for students. Can you imagine getting in your car and telling your GPS app, "Let's go"? That's like beginning a lesson without a clear objective. In the same way, if the driver prefers a route that takes a bit longer, the app needs to know that, or it will take you via the fastest route by default. If the vehicle is almost out of gas, the app can't guess that the driver needs to stop at a station; a stop must be added to trip. An invaluable trait of most GPS apps is anticipating confusion. "Stay in the outermost left lane to turn at the light" signals to the driver that they will be making a right turn soon after a left turn. Likewise, "Go through this light and turn at the next left" tells the driver that there may be someplace they need to stop or pause before making the next turn.

The same is true with learning objectives and formative assessment. Students need a clearly defined outcome for their learning as they begin. Even in inquiry-based learning, students must know what is expected of them (thinking skills, general outcomes, or direction). Furthermore, a wide range of research indicates a high correlation between clear communication of goals and goal criteria with high academic achievement (effect size = 0.85; Hattie, 2024) (Biggs et al., 2022; Hattie, 2023; Saphier et al., 2025).

To successfully navigate the learning, students must understand the outcome and the critical "stop lights" or measurement criteria they'll meet along the way. Almarode and colleagues (2021) define these steps and possible moments for assessment as success criteria. In physics, a possible *moment* might be the rotational effect of a force on a body around a fixed point or axis—like the movement of a pushed door on its hinges when opened. Defining the assessment criteria for students is like telling them how far and how hard they will need to push to open the door to their new learning. Without that information, they won't know how close they are getting or how much more effort they need to exert to reach the outcome. Without such signposts, learning is often vague, and it is easy for students to lose their way or give up entirely.

Use Formative Assessment

Implement ongoing checks for understanding to tailor instruction. Much has been written about formative assessment (see Chapter 3), but sticking with the "moment" definition and door analogy from the previous strategy, formative evaluation aims to in*form* the teacher about which students are successfully opening the door and which need a different approach or more muscle to push the door open. As Saphier and colleagues (2025, p. 550) put it, "Assessment that is designed to increase student achievement is crafted to accomplish three goals:

- Motivate students to want to do better.
- Give students useful information they can use to do better.

- Inform teachers' reteaching plans so students can do better."

Formative assessment gives teachers a quick and clear picture of how students are doing, highlighting who's understanding the lesson and who might need extra help or a different approach to keep moving ahead. To ensure assessments hit the mark, the following strategies include practical, easy-to-use ideas for designing effective formative assessment in your classroom. As you go through these strategies, remember that useful assessment always starts with careful planning. A strong formative assessment doesn't just measure progress; it also sparks students' interest, gathers valuable feedback (from the teacher or even their peers), and highlights areas you might need to revisit. To make this happen, watch students' responses closely and offer feedback they can immediately use.

When formative assessment hits the mark, it generates "small data"—bite-sized insights into student learning—that help both teacher and students see the next steps forward.

- **Signal Spectrum:** The teacher should encourage students to use clear hand gestures when sharing their answers. For example, ask them to hold up one finger if they pick option *A*, two fingers for option *B*, and so forth. For quick checks of understanding or agreement, they could also simply show a thumbs-up for *yes* or a thumbs-down for *no*. Encourage students to discuss their signals with a partner before showing them to the teacher. Target individual or small groups of students for one-on-one interactions.

- **Card Colors:** Colored cards can be distributed to students, with each color representing a different response. For example, green is for *yes*, red is for *no*, and yellow is for *unsure*. Students are asked to explain their choice to a peer before holding up their card. Students' responses uncover misconceptions or trend errors.

- **Post-It Palette:** Students use two different colored sticky notes stuck back-to-back. They show one color for one response and flip it to show the other color for a different response. Students discuss their color choice with a partner and then share it with the class. The teacher notes class trends and identifies individual students to follow up with for more in-depth discussions.
- **Stick Signals:** Students can also use craft sticks painted in different colors. Each color corresponds to a different answer or level of understanding. Students pair up and compare their stick choices before showing them to the teacher. Look for trends and speak to students one-on-one if they are consistently incorrect.
- **Card Codes:** Students employ playing cards to indicate their responses. Different suits, numbers, or face cards are assigned different meanings. Students discuss their card choice with a classmate before showing it.
- **Mini Boards:** The teacher provides mini whiteboards, chalkboards, or gel pads for students to write their answers on and hold up for the teacher and the class to see. Students share and compare their responses with a partner before holding them up. Feedback allows groups or individuals to know if they are moving in the right direction or need to make corrections.
- **Paper Responses:** Students write their answers on plain paper, which the teacher quickly reviews as they circulate around the room. Students can exchange papers with a peer for feedback before responses are collected.
- **Quick Practice:** Students work on a few problems or questions from the textbook while the teacher walks around to check the initial responses. They then discuss their answers with a neighbor. The teacher solicits answer rationales while roaming around the room and checking students' responses.

- **Padlet Polls:** Students go to a link to a Padlet or other online poll that allows them to write their answers with a justification. They discuss their chosen option with a partner before displaying it. The teacher looks for class trends and highlights them for the class.

- **Exit Insights:** At the end of a lesson, students write down one thing they learned and one question they still have. The teacher collects students' thoughts as they leave the classroom to gauge understanding and plan future lessons quickly. Students share their insights with a peer before handing them in. During the next class session, the teacher will provide a review for targeted small-group reteaching or clarification.

- **Peer Reviews:** Students assess one another's work using a simple rubric. This can provide immediate feedback and promote collaborative learning. The teacher encourages students to discuss their peers' work and feedback.

- **Pair and Share:** The teacher poses a question to the class and has students think about their answer, discuss their ideas with a partner, and share their responses with the group. This approach promotes deeper reflection and provides an opportunity to gauge student understanding by listening in on discussions. Figure 7.2 shows a sample rubric to guide and evaluate student responses during pair-and-share activities.

- **Speedy Quizzes:** Short, timed quizzes assess student understanding quickly. These can be paper-based or digital, using tools such as Wayground or Socrative. After the quiz, students can discuss their answers with a peer. This opportunity pulls out common errors to discuss as a class.

- **Notebook Reflections:** Students maintain notebooks in which they complete quick reflections or answer questions about the lesson. The teacher reviews these notebooks periodically to assess understanding and provide more detailed feedback. Encourage students to share their reflections with a partner.

Figure 7.2 Sample Rubric for Pair and Share

Criteria	Exemplary (4)	Proficient (3)	Developing (2)	Beginning (1)
Engagement	Actively listens and enthusiastically participates in the discussion.	Actively listens and regularly participates in the discussion.	Occasionally listens and participates minimally in the discussion.	Rarely listens and shows little to no participation.
Content Understanding	Clearly and accurately communicates a detailed understanding of content or concepts.	Communicates a general understanding of the content or concepts.	Communicates a partial or somewhat unclear understanding of the content or concepts.	Demonstrates minimal or incorrect understanding of the content or concepts.
Communication Clarity	Speaks audibly and uses appropriate vocabulary consistently.	Usually speaks clearly and uses appropriate vocabulary.	Speaks somewhat clearly; vocabulary is occasionally appropriate.	Difficult to understand; uses unclear or inappropriate vocabulary.
Interaction with Partner	Engages respectfully, builds on ideas, provides evidence-based counterpoints, and encourages participation.	Interacts respectfully, sometimes building upon the partner's ideas or providing evidence-based counterarguments.	Limited interaction; seldom builds upon the partner's ideas or provides counterarguments	Little to no meaningful interaction; may disregard partner's contributions; provides no counterargument

- **Concept Maps:** Students create a concept map of what they learned. This visual representation helps them arrange their thoughts and reveals how well they understand the connections between concepts. Students compare their map with a peer's map. Collect maps from target students for more in-depth discussions and feedback.

- **Minute Summaries:** Before the teacher wraps up class, students quickly jot down the main points they learned—just a short, one-minute note. This simple activity helps them lock in key ideas and gives the teacher a quick check on how well they've understood the lesson. Afterward, students can swap their notes with peers or hand them in for quick feedback and follow-up.

- **Digital Surveys:** Digital tools such as Poll Everywhere or Google Forms can be used to conduct instant polls or surveys. These tools provide immediate feedback and help gauge student understanding. Students discuss the poll results in small groups.

- **Pitstop Exit Slips:** Students do these right after guided practice as brief opportunities to pause and reflect. Using small pieces of paper or note cards, students respond to Depth of Knowledge (DOK) level 2 or higher questions. (See Figure 7.3 for examples.) For instance, if students are solving a math problem, they might use three key mathematical terms to explain their solution in writing. When discussing historical events, such as the causes of World War I, students can justify their reasoning about why a particular incident led to conflict. Even younger students can participate. After reading or listening to a story, they might write a complete sentence identifying the funniest character, including an example of what made that character humorous. Exit slips typically occur at the end of the lesson, but pitstop exit slips offer a mid-lesson formative assessment opportunity.

Figure 7.3   Graphic for Webb's Depth of Knowledge (DoK)

Aspect	DoK Level 1: Basic Recall	DoK Level 2: Skill & Concept Application	DoK Level 3: Strategic Thinking & Reasoning	DoK Level 4: Extended Thinking & Investigation
Cognitive Demand	Recalling facts, terms, or procedures.	Applying skills & concepts, requires some processing.	Reasoning, planning, & complex thinking.	Investigating & synthesizing over an extended time.
Type of Answer	One correct answer.	One correct answer; may involve multiple steps.	Multiple possible answers or approaches.	Multiple possible answers & approaches.
Key Characteristics	Simple recall or execution.	Engages mental processes beyond recall.	Requires justification, planning, & evidence.	Involves multiple steps & extended effort.
Examples	• Perform basic arithmetic operations. • List steps of the water cycle. • Recall dates & events from history. • Identify main characters in a story. • Analyze & list key events of the American Revolution.	• Summarize a story or article. • Classify different rocks based on their properties. • Explain the reasoning behind a scientific phenomenon. • Identify a basic inference from a story. • Identify motivations of a story's main character. • Analyze & explain the process of photosynthesis. • Analyze & explain the causes of World War I in bullet points.	• Design an experiment to test a hypothesis. • Interpret data to make predictions. • Construct a logical argument based on evidence. • Identify the moral of a story. • Identify symbols in *The Catcher in The Rye* & discuss their significance. • Analyze data from a plant growth experiment & draw conclusions about effects of different variables. • Analyze Civil Rights Movement primary source documents to determine perspectives of different stakeholders.	• Conduct a research project spanning several weeks. • Develop a business plan for a project. • Identify motifs & themes across multiple texts & produce a comparative analysis essay. • Identify & analyze differing perspectives on the American Dream portrayed in *Of Mice & Men & The Joy Luck Club.* • Analyze & evaluate the impact of deforestation on local ecosystems & propose mitigation solutions.

Source: Data from WebbAlign (2024), https://www.webbalign.org/about/dok-explained

- **Tech Cards:** Plickers cards—printed response cards with unique QR-like patterns that a teacher scans with a smartphone for instant feedback—are useful for quick, tech-enabled formative assessment. Students hold up cards with unique patterns that are scanned with a smartphone to instantly collect and view their responses. Students can compare their responses with a partner before showing them.
- **Fishbowl Chats:** A preorganized small group of students discusses a topic while the rest of the class observes. Rotate groups to ensure everyone participates. This method allows assessment of understanding through direct observation and peer interaction. Students provide feedback on the discussion. A variation of this is the Sidekick, where a student sits behind or next to each student in a speaking role and can perform quick research and pass notes to the speaker.
- **Traffic Lights:** Students use red, yellow, and green cups. Students place the cups on their desks to indicate their understanding: green for complete understanding, yellow for partial understanding, and red for confusion. This visual signal allows the teacher to identify who needs help quickly. Students can discuss their color choices with a neighbor and the teacher.
- **Rubrics for Clarity:** Teacher-developed detailed rubrics provide consistent grading standards. Students compare their product to the rubric's attributes for a self-check. Circulate and confirm or discuss the self-assessment.

It is worth noting again that, although these strategies can help check for understanding, their impact depends on how they're used. Saphier and colleagues (2025) remind us that assessment supports achievement only when it inspires students to improve, offers them clear guidance, and shapes what the teacher does next. For these benefits to take hold, teachers must pay close attention to how each student responds and then provide specific and actionable feedback. When used this way, formative assessment yields small but powerful insights or "small data" points that help drive learning forward, moment by moment, and potentially affect student academic performance (effect size = 0.92; Hattie, 2024).

Provide Positive and Constructive Feedback

Feedback is the breakfast of champions in the classroom; it nourishes students' growth by telling them what they're doing well and where they can improve. Effective feedback goes beyond a simple "Good job" or a checkmark; it explicitly highlights the performance and guides the student on the next steps (Biggs et al., 2022; Hattie, 2023; Saphier et al., 2025). In practice, this might look like a middle school language arts teacher writing comments on a draft essay: "Your introduction grabs attention—nice work! For the next draft, try to provide more evidence in the second paragraph to support your argument." It could also be verbal: "I notice you solved that problem using a clever method. If you try that approach on the next question, I bet you'll find it easier."

The key is that feedback is timely and actionable. Rather than simply pointing out errors, the teacher frames feedback constructively, almost like a coach advising an athlete in the middle of a game or an instructor encouraging or correcting a student in the middle of a piano lesson. Regular feedback helps students stay motivated and understand how to improve academically or behaviorally. When students get this type of guidance consistently, it gradually shapes their approach and encourages them to tweak their methods and put in more effective effort.

Offer Retake Opportunities

Allow students to retake assessments to demonstrate learning improvement. Not everyone learns at the same rate; some have to push harder on the door to get to the learning. An AP student once expressed dismay that a peer was allowed to retake a test and possibly achieve an *A*. Angela asked what bothered them about this. They said, "I got an *A* the first time the test was given; it doesn't seem fair that my grade and my peer's grade will be the same." They continued to talk until Angela asked, "So even though your peer now knows as much as you do, you think they should not be recognized for that?" The student was confused at first and then said, "I guess I never really think about grades being about learning and growth. They are just a competitive thing for me. School would be better if it changed how we think about grades."

Retake assessments can be rearranged or reformatted to make sure they measure true understanding rather than simple recall. For example, when a student retakes a test, the teacher might change question order, wording, or context, so students must apply or provide more in-depth justifications about what they've learned instead of repeating memorized answers. This keeps the process authentic and fair—especially in light of the AP student's reaction in the earlier story—because it shows that earning a high grade isn't about luck or competition but about genuinely mastering the material, even if it takes more than one attempt.

Reflect and Revise

Grading methods should be continuously evaluated to ensure fairness. After every summative assessment, the teacher needs to take time to look at the results individually and as a class and ask themselves these questions:

- "Do these grades reflect what I thought about the learning? Are there any surprises?" If formative assessment has been used regularly throughout the learning, there should not be surprises.

- "Am I seeing growth, or are students consistently getting the same grades?" Lack of growth may signal a need for a different instructional strategy.
- "Were there specific areas where multiple students made errors? Do I need to go back and clear up misconceptions? How can I do that before the assessment next time? Do I need to fill the holes in their learning before I go on?"
- "Did my assessment measure what I intended it to assess? Are my questions at the right level of complexity?"

Give Open-Book Assessments

Open-book exams encourage knowledge application. It is essential to think about what learning is being tested. If the desired outcome is for students to use information from a text to answer a higher-level thinking question, then the option for an open-book test may be exactly right. For example, suppose students learning about anatomy and physiology are asked what injuries they should look for after a fall and how they should be prioritized. In that case, the names of the bones or other identifying body parts are not the priority; knowing the crucial steps for assessing injuries will be what the students should demonstrate. Using the book will allow them to use correct academic vocabulary as they work. In another example, students may be asked how the author uses diction to develop a theme. They would be able to answer the question best by using the text rather than trying to memorize specific passages.

Provide Narrative Reports

Narrative feedback adds important insights to traditional grades. During independent practice, students meet with the teacher either individually or in small groups to discuss specific aspects of their learning. The meetings are collaborative, so students feel they are partners in their education and realize they own their growth.

In an elementary classroom, narrative reports might sound like a brief conversation about reading or math progress: "You've grown so much in identifying main ideas. Next week, let's practice finding supporting details to make your summaries stronger." The teacher might jot this note into the student's learning folder, share it with families through a progress log, or provide it in the context of small-group work on common skill building. Younger students benefit from hearing clear, descriptive language about their learning rather than just seeing a score, and they begin to connect effort with growth.

In a secondary classroom, narrative feedback might take the form of written conference notes or short goal-setting meetings. For instance, in a high school science class, a teacher might tell a student, "Your data collection is precise, but your conclusion needs to connect more directly to your hypothesis. Let's work on that in your next lab." The teacher might summarize progress in an English class in a short paragraph: "Your voice as a writer is becoming more confident. Continue to vary your sentence openings and strengthen your transitions between paragraphs." Nowadays, it is not uncommon to see more secondary teachers pulling small groups of students during a lesson to focus on common errors or shore up missing foundational skills in 10- to 15-minute segments—a perfect setting for delivering explicit narrative feedback.

In elementary and secondary settings, narrative reports provide students with specific, actionable feedback beyond numbers or letters. They turn grading into a dialogue about progress, helping students see where they've been successful, where they need to grow, and what concrete steps will move them forward.

Use Oral Assessments

Verbal presentations serve as an alternative assessment format. Verbal presentations often encourage students who struggle to articulate themselves in writing to shine. However, not all students are comfortable in front of an audience. Consider allowing students to present to a small audience, such as a group of five. Allow them to rehearse their responses before speaking in front of the class or group. This practice ensures that all students, especially those who are more introverted or are struggling with the target language, can participate meaningfully. Rehearsal promotes equity by giving every student a voice. Ritchhart and Church (2020) provide several strategies for encouraging rehearsal in the classroom, such as peer rehearsing before presenting to a small group or the whole class, using sentence starters or paragraph frames to help students articulate their thoughts as they practice presenting to peers, and practicing summaries or opinion pieces before presenting full-blown arguments.

Long-Term, High-Prep Strategies

Use Goal-Tracking Tools

Students can use tools to monitor their progress. In some classrooms, teachers give students progressive rubrics that delineate process steps such as "entering," "maturing," "advancing," and "excelling." Students determine when they move from one rubric to another and give the teacher input on where they think they fall. Writing teachers can use this type of rubric to help all students monitor growth, no matter where they enter. Both rubrics (effect size = 0.52) and self- and teacher feedback (effect size = 0.50) potentially lead to high student academic achievement (Hattie, 2024).

Deliver Competency-Based Assessments

Focus assessments on skill mastery rather than traditional grading. Traditional grading practices, such as "the curve," do not communicate whether a student has mastered the objective or learning expectations. Reviewing grading practices to ensure they reflect student learning and understanding is crucial. Consider how different assessment methods more accurately measure learning for all students. This approach promotes equity in evaluating student performance. Feldman (2023) provides valuable insights on equitable grading practices in *Grading for Equity*.

In addition, it's important to educate students about the purpose and methods of grading. Help them understand the difference between academic learning and completing assignments. This knowledge empowers students to take ownership of their learning and promotes equity in their academic journey. What does this look like in action?

In a 4th grade math unit on multidigit multiplication, instead of using a single unit test with a traditional percentage grade, the teacher can break the standard into competencies: understanding place value, setting up the algorithm correctly, and interpreting word problems involving multiplication. Each student receives a checklist that outlines these specific skills, and they are assessed through a mix of activities that include hands-on math stations, short formative quizzes, and one-on-one math talks. Students are rated on each competency on a scale from "not yet" to "approaching" to "meets" to "exceeds."

If a student doesn't master a skill, they receive targeted feedback and additional support (like small-group instruction) before reassessment. No penalties are given for needing extra time. Progress is shared with families using student-friendly learning reports, not letter grades. Students are also asked to reflect on what they've learned and set new goals for growth. This approach removes the pressure of grades, encourages an effort-based mindset, and focuses on mastering the learning objectives rather than accumulating points for tasks.

As another example, consider a 10th grade English class working on argumentative essays. Rather than assigning a single percentage grade based on grammar, format, and deadline, the teacher can build a competency-based rubric tied directly to the standards: crafting a strong thesis, using textual evidence, organizing ideas clearly, and revising based on feedback. Students are introduced to the rubric at the beginning of the unit and practice each skill with mini-assessments and peer feedback. As students submit drafts, the teacher provides targeted, skill-specific feedback; allows revisions without penalty; and occasionally provides whole-class lessons if everyone struggles with the same concept. The teacher assesses each skill individually on a scale from "developing" to "proficient" to "advanced."

Grades are reported by competency, not by assignment, and students can see where they have grown or still need support. The teacher holds brief conferences with students individually or in smaller groups to explain how the progress on the assessments reflects actual learning—not just compliance or completion. This method shifts the focus from a collection of points or grade letters to authentic skill development, helping students understand that grades should reflect what they've learned, not how quickly they complete tasks. It also promotes equity by valuing mastery over speed or prior preparation.

Organize Collaborative Grading Sessions

Align grading practices with colleagues for consistency. Teachers often use common planning time to organize this collaborative grading. The most successful of these sessions is when each teacher brings student artifacts with names redacted. Teachers take a stack of papers and decide if they "meet," "approach," or "fall below" the standard they assessed. Once the artifacts are sorted, a facilitator asks the teachers to look at one stack at a time, discuss what that group demonstrates, and decide what learning steps they need next.

One day, Keith observed a group of teachers who completed this process for the first time. One paper in the "meets" stack was different from the others in that it clearly did not demonstrate mastery of the standard. The teachers talked about why it might have been put there. Finally, a team member chimed in and said, "That student is in my class and was in my stack to assess. I am sitting here realizing that I have a preconceived notion that their work will meet standards. Their work is always very neat and on time, and they stay on task and work hard. Now, as I look at it, I realize that without this process, I would continue to miss what they need to grow and learn. Although I am thoroughly embarrassed, I am so grateful that we did this!"

Use Multiple Measures

Effective teachers act like detectives, gathering clues about each student's strengths and areas of need from various sources. Rather than relying on just one test or summative score, a teacher might review quizzes, classwork, and observations. For example, a math teacher might examine homework, verbal comments, and a short quiz to identify why a student struggles with fractions. By contrast, an English teacher might combine AI-assisted reading assessments with one-on-one conferences to understand a reader's comprehension skills. Research supports this comprehensive approach; using multiple data points leads to better-informed teaching decisions (McLeskey et al., 2017). Just as a doctor uses various data points (e.g., blood work, X-rays, patient input, patient history) to make an accurate diagnosis, a teacher uses all the information available to diagnose how to help a student learn best.

Use Data as Your Dashboard

When assessment data reveal that students haven't yet grasped a concept, it's easy for teachers to feel discouraged or even take it personally. Instead, consider data as a classroom's dashboard, just like the fuel gauge on a car. When the indicator shows an almost empty tank, the driver doesn't get upset or blame themselves for missing it sooner. They wouldn't put a smiley face sticker over it and keep driving, either. Instead, they'd simply plan their next stop to refuel.

In the same way, think of student assessment results as signals guiding the teaching journey. Data don't judge or criticize; rather, they should inform a teacher's next move. The signs shouldn't be ignored or blamed on oneself or others, and frustration shouldn't "take the wheel." Data are best used to indicate when it's time to adjust the teaching approach or try a new strategy. Keeping this mindset will empower the teacher and set up students for more tremendous success.

Assessment is more than a checkpoint—it's a conversation about learning. When teachers use feedback, goal tracking, and multiple measures to reveal what students truly understand, grades become learning tools rather than labels. By emphasizing mastery over speed and progress over perfection, educators create classrooms where assessment drives growth rather than anxiety. Every formative check, rubric discussion, or student conference becomes a chance to affirm that learning is an evolving process—and that every learner can move forward with clarity, confidence, and purpose.

Teacher Burnout and Stress

Teachers often face overwhelming stress, and the demands of teaching and managing parental, student, and administrative involvement can lead to burnout. This chapter is all about essential self-care practices, which indirectly support student outcomes by enhancing teacher retention, morale, and emotional health. More notably, the repeated emphasis in this chapter on structured professional learning communities (PLCs) and collaborative reflection aligns directly with collective teacher efficacy (effect size = 1.01), which Hattie (2024) identified as the highest-ranked influence on student academic achievement.

To maximize student learning, educators should continue prioritizing structured instruction and learning-focused collaborations—such as professional learning communities PLCs, reflection pods, peer mentoring, and responsive instructional adaptations—while clearly distinguishing them from broader wellness initiatives. This chapter provides more than 80 restorative strategies for building supportive networks, establishing healthy boundaries, and accessing professional support systems, all of which help teachers thrive both professionally and personally. To help implement them, the strategies in this chapter are grouped into three categories according to their required level of effort and planning:

- Immediate, Low-Prep Strategies
- Routine, Moderate-Prep Strategies
- Long-Term, High-Prep Strategies

Immediate, Low-Prep Strategies

Engage in Self-Care

Attending thoughtfully designed self-care workshops provides teachers with access to culturally attuned, research-based wellness techniques that are easily integrated into their daily routines. For example, teachers might learn brief mindfulness exercises influenced by Indigenous practices or experiment with short sessions of yoga or qigong to relieve tension during a planning period. All of these are approaches supported by emerging evidence on the benefits of mindful movement (Goldberg et al., 2018; Kabat-Zinn, 1990; Ratey & Manning, 2018). Guided journaling, even in 5- to 10-minute bursts throughout the day, can help teachers process challenging interactions and reframe them more constructively (Pennebaker & Smyth, 2016).

These "go-to" strategies are ones some educators seamlessly weave into their daily schedules. For example, one New York City kindergarten teacher introduced a yoga routine led by his students as part of their daily morning meetings. Each yoga pose matched a letter, helping students practice letter names while also getting some gentle exercise. The teacher noticed that students—and even he—often arrived carrying leftover stress from earlier that morning or the night before. Beginning the day with yoga helped melt away that stress, making it easier for everyone to ease into class feeling calm and ready to learn.

In addition, self-care workshops that include hands-on activities—such as taking a short walk outside or cooking together as a group—can show teachers practical ways to add relaxing and restorative moments to their busy weeks. Teachers who experience simple forest therapy sessions during a workshop are more likely to take a short walk outdoors during lunch. Several studies suggest people only need short doses, or about 10 minutes of walking or sitting in nature, for a positive impact (White et al., 2023). At the same time, those who learn stress-relief cooking techniques experiment with quick, nutritious meal preparations at home. When self-care is presented as a set of adaptable, everyday practices rather than a one-time event, teachers are empowered to integrate wellness into the fabric of their professional lives (White et al., 2023).

Work with Peer Mentors

Instead of thinking about mentorship as a one-way relationship where a more experienced teacher imparts knowledge to a newer teacher, imagine a partnership in which both colleagues support each other's overall well-being. For example, just as someone might team up with a colleague to stay on track with a fitness goal, a teacher can also find a "wellness check-in" partner to share stress-relief ideas regularly. During brief chats or scheduled meetups, the pair might discuss simple strategies such as logging off from work emails at a set time (digital detoxing), journaling about challenging classroom moments, or taking short nature walks during breaks (Nguyen et al., 2022; Pennebaker, 1997). By openly talking about mental health and coping strategies, peer relationships become sources of ongoing emotional support, ensuring that educators feel understood, balanced, and a bit more equipped to handle the demands of the school day.

Review Your Time Management

Shake things up a bit. Instead of always leaning on classic tools like planners, timers, and checklists, try something a little different. Ever heard of the "green-yellow-red" method? Rather than ranking tasks by deadline or urgency, sort them based on how much mental energy they need (Nieuwhof, 2021). For example, green activities might be energizing, like designing a fun outdoor lesson. Yellow tasks are those routine things a teacher neither dreads nor loves, like grading regular assignments. Red tasks drain energy fast, like tackling complicated school improvement paperwork or writing a grant proposal. Thinking about daily tasks as a mix of colors can help teachers manage their emotional and mental energy in a fresh, practical way. Give it a go!

Use AI in Moderation

Innovative time management also involves leveraging technology in moderation. Using AI-driven tools can help automate low-level tasks, allowing teachers to reserve their prime mental hours for meaningful student interactions (Burns, 2024; Kraft & Papay, 2020). Strategic delegation with AI tools saves time and conserves emotional bandwidth, preventing cumulative stress and contributing to long-term well-being. Some examples of low-level tasks that AI could help teachers automate include

- **Grading routine assignments:** For instance, an AI tool could quickly score multiple-choice quizzes or basic math drills, reducing time spent on manual grading.
- **Generating basic practice materials:** AI-driven platforms can create worksheets, vocabulary lists, differentiated texts by Lexile score, or simple reading comprehension questions aligned to a given text, saving the teacher from starting these resources from scratch.
- **Sorting and organizing student data:** Even though many teachers have data dashboards and more data analysis than they need, some do not. Instead of manually entering attendance records, homework submissions, or test scores, an AI tool could compile and categorize this information, freeing the teacher to focus on more explicit feedback or small-group reteaching.
- **Automating email or announcement templates:** AI chatbots or email assistants can draft and schedule routine messages, such as homework reminders or field trip updates, freeing the teacher to focus on more substantive communication.

Consider Counseling Services

Rather than seeing counseling as a last resort, normalize regular mental health check-ins by partnering with community counseling centers or adopting tele-mental health services accessible from home. Seek out providers with "open-door" virtual support sessions, where you can anonymously drop in for short consultations to ensure that help is always within reach, breaking the stigma around seeking emotional help (Hwang et al., 2020). Nowadays, many school districts offer virtual and video chat counseling as part of their employee assistance program benefits.

Try Tech Wellness Programs

Incorporating technology-based wellness challenges—like friendly step competitions, daily emailed inspirational quotes, or short guided meditation sessions delivered via a mobile app—enhances participation and engagement. Recent evidence shows that digital wellness programs effectively support employee and teacher well-being by combining physical activity tracking and mindfulness tools within accessible platforms (Economides et al., 2018; Thai et al., 2023). By tapping into digital innovation, a wellness program can become a multifaceted support system that resonates with a variety of personal preferences and backgrounds.

Journal

Developed over decades, James Pennebaker's writings are considered the cornerstone of expressive writing. The third edition of his most popular text, *Opening Up by Writing It Down*, offers multiple benefits of writing for self-care (Pennebaker & Smyth, 2016):

- **Health Benefits:** Writing about stressful or traumatic experiences can lead to measurable physical and mental health improvements. Such benefits include fewer doctor visits, improved immune functioning, reduced symptoms of depression, and better overall well-being.
- **Meaning Making:** Putting emotions and events into language helps individuals organize and understand their experiences.

This process allows them to reframe and make sense of difficult memories and ultimately integrate these experiences into their life stories in a less distressing way.

- **Broad Applicability:** The benefits of expressive writing are not limited to individuals with major trauma. It also helps people cope with everyday stressors, relationship issues, workplace conflicts, and transitions. Moreover, writing interventions can be adapted in length, frequency, and format to suit different individuals and contexts.

When journaling for expression, consider multiple prompts. Over the years, several teachers have suggested the following general prompts: Write to... make a decision, solve a problem, analyze a relationship or classroom issue, generate ideas, vent, reflect on your progress, or celebrate a success.

Know and Prepare for Your Triggers

Educators benefit from understanding their emotional triggers: the specific words, situations, or behaviors that prompt an intense, often negative, reaction. What unsettles one teacher is different from what affects another. For example, though one teacher might feel rattled by constant interruptions during a lesson, another may remain unbothered but become stressed by last-minute schedule changes. Recognizing these personal, emotional hot spots allows educators to prepare in advance. By having simple, ready-to-use remedies on hand—such as taking a brief mental break, practicing a calming breathing exercise, or having a supportive phrase ready to remind themselves of their purpose—they can prevent emotional upheaval from derailing their teaching and collegial interactions (Nicholson et al., 2019).

Routine, Moderate-Prep Strategies

Build Alliances

Building alliances goes beyond simple collegiality; it involves forging mutual support circles that celebrate successes, openly share best practices, and encourage vulnerability. Teachers might create reflection pods where small groups meet regularly, either in person or virtually, to discuss current challenges and brainstorm solutions that have worked in other cultural or educational contexts (Sarason et al., 1990). These pods can incorporate a social contract that ensures confidentiality, trust, and respect, allowing teachers to connect on a deeper level and reduce feelings of isolation in demanding school environments. Structured professional collaboration leads to one of the highest teacher impacts on student academic achievement: collective teacher efficacy (effect size = 1.01; Hattie, 2024).

A professional learning community (PLC) might meet the criteria for strong teacher alliance, but that depends on what the PLC regularly accomplishes. An authentic PLC is a group of teachers who regularly collaborate to analyze student performance and plan effective teaching strategies to enhance learning outcomes. An example of such a group occurred in a Southern California school where Tamarra, Angie, and Keith worked. We observed a very high-functioning PLC. The 2nd grade teachers spent the first half of the meeting looking at student artifacts and discussing what the results meant for their instruction. The trust among the teachers was evident as they made themselves vulnerable and gave examples of what they struggled with in teaching the current standard.

Together, they planned the next lesson, focusing first on the students who were progressing as expected and then spinning off from that for those who were not progressing as expected and those who were progressing at a higher rate than expected. They agreed on some basics for each group, and then each teacher volunteered to write an upcoming lesson plan for one of the three groups. They would practice what they called "the dance of the thumb drive" (where they passed around the shared lessons) the following day, giving them time to ask one another questions before the lesson. They truly believed in their ability to work together and meet every student's needs.

Plan Flexibly

Teachers can adopt agile instructional models, allowing responsive pacing and content adjustments. These approaches borrow ideas from strategies such as "just-in-time" teaching and adaptive learning technology. They help teachers quickly shift their lessons based on changing student needs, reducing frustration and avoiding extra work (Xu & Carless, 2021). For example, a teacher might pause halfway through class to give students a quick check-in quiz. Using those results, the teacher can then gather a small group of students who need extra help while the rest of the class continues working on their own. This way, teachers can provide focused support without interrupting the rhythm of the whole class.

Other teachers embed reflective pauses for themselves—perhaps guided by journaling prompts—that can help identify what's genuinely effective, reducing stress and preventing burnout (Schön, 1983). For example, one passionate science teacher started closing each lesson with a quick reflective writing activity. As her students briefly noted what they grasped and where they still felt unsure, she used those moments to jot down her own thoughts about the lesson. She captured her thoughts about which parts of the lesson went well, what areas needed improvement, and ideas for adjustments she could make next time. This simple addition allowed her to maintain a healthier perspective, keep frustrations at bay, and focus her energy where it mattered most: improving instruction for her students.

Review Your Circles of Influence

One innovative approach to managing stress involves focusing energy on what's within the teacher's circle of influence rather than fixating on uncontrollable factors (Covey, 2020; Young et al., 2023). Use simple drawings to mentally map out personal realms of influence—lesson planning, classroom relationships, mindset, time management—and differentiate those activities or dispositions from external pressures such as district policies, state requirements, or unpredictable administrative demands. By engaging in this activity, teachers can better manage their emotional energy and put their effort into areas where they can truly make a difference.

These circles of influence also lend themselves well to team activities; educators can bring their maps to meetings and discuss them, helping one another pinpoint practical ways to tackle shared challenges. Over time, this collective focus fosters a culture of empowerment in which educators celebrate small but meaningful victories that lie within their control. Check out how we've seen this same strategy used with students and a visual of this concept in Chapter 1, p. 19).

This simple activity led to a breakthrough for one frustrated math teacher. A math department chair and Mensa member known for solving complex equations in his head, he was nearly undone by what he considered "incompetent administration." Constant protocol changes and poor leadership from the principal consumed his mental space and overshadowed his accomplishments, leaving him on edge and increasingly frustrated. During a department meeting, his instructional coach introduced circles of influence. Initially skeptical, the teacher listed sources of his stress—unruly students, outdated textbooks, limited technology, low test scores, and the "useless principal"—and placed each item according to his degree of control.

This written and visual sorting activity led to a powerful realization. Even though he still felt bothered by his principal's shortcomings, he clearly saw that the administrator occupied just a small spot at the edge of his influence. With this fresh insight, he shifted his attention toward areas where he truly had control: supporting student learning, strengthening his team, and enhancing his lessons. To this day, he will tell anyone interested that this simple activity helped him shed much of the anger and frustration that once consumed him. He embraced a pragmatic understanding that he couldn't change the principal but could change his own response, ultimately finding empowerment and greater professional satisfaction.

Set Boundaries

Practice saying *no* to extra demands or negotiate more reasonable deadlines with administrators. Try writing a personal mission statement. Why? Clearly stating what a healthy work–life balance means to you can simplify your daily choices. Instead of second-guessing personal decisions, the mission statement will provide a helpful guide to follow. Borrowed from both psychology and the business world, strategies such as this can help you protect your personal well-being without guilt—or worry about consequences (Shockley et al., 2021). Another innovative twist is integrating "boundary buddies"—colleagues who hold one another accountable for not overextending themselves. To that end, they send reminders to shut down their computers at a reasonable hour and encourage one another to skip unnecessary weekend emails. Over time, these community-based safeguards may embed boundary awareness into the team's culture, making it easier for everyone to respect personal limits (Covey, 2020).

Use Tactics for Managing Challenging Adult Behaviors

Deal with difficult adults—be they administrators or colleagues—by adapting techniques from conflict resolution. Managing challenging professional relationships isn't just about maintaining harmony; it's also a key stress-reduction strategy for educators. Unresolved tension among adults can drain emotional energy and spill over into classroom performance. By approaching conflicts with calm, clarity, and structure, teachers can preserve their focus for what matters most: supporting students.

The following are a handful of quick tactics recommended by Young and colleagues (2023):

- **Set norms.** Establishing agreed-upon expectations at the outset helps ensure everyone knows their professional interactions' focus, scope, and limits. Instead of stale team norms like "Show up on time," try norms that address real problems. For example, if people continually talk over one another, discuss this as a group and try a group norm for "sharing airtime." In a district in Nevada, the leadership team was hamstrung by the discord between two of its members. Meetings were purposely avoided, and when they did occur, limited positive progress was hampered by the two members intentionally sabotaging ideas supported by the other. Tamarra came in as a new facilitator and helped the group establish norms—one of which was "positive presupposition that others are doing the best they can." Tamarra assigned each member to be the keeper of a norm who would define the norm for the rest of the group. One of the two disputants became "keeper of positive presupposition." When she tried to define it, she broke down in tears and said, "This is all I have ever wanted from [the other teacher], and it seems impossible. I can't be the keeper of this!" The other teacher responded with "I want the same thing from you!" Tamarra suggested they leave the room and discuss their feelings with the norm in mind. Several minutes later, they came in, arm in arm, with tear-streaked faces and apologized to the group for their behavior.

The meeting continued quite successfully. Norms can be very powerful.

- **Find common ground.** Emphasizing shared goals and values—such as student success—helps move the conversation toward consensus and away from personal disagreement. Dozens of teams we've observed maintained success with this focus when they brought actual student work to the team meetings—student writing, working math problems, lab notebooks, and so on. A mountain of student work isn't necessary for a fruitful conversation; start small by sampling the artifacts of high-, medium-, and low-performing students from each class or course.

- **Clarify.** Asking for definitions or clarifications prevents misunderstandings and keeps discussions focused on concrete issues rather than vague complaints or assumptions. Discovering what a colleague means when using terms like *mastery, formative assessment,* or *student engagement* might be surprising. Discuss the vague notions and reach an agreement on commonly used lingo.

- **Dignify differences.** Acknowledging that multiple philosophies or approaches can exist in education shows respect for colleagues' perspectives while maintaining a focus on the collective goals. In schools, differences in teaching philosophy are inevitable—one teacher may favor structured, teacher-led lessons while another leans toward inquiry-based learning or project work. Instead of viewing these contrasts as conflicts, dignifying differences means recognizing that each approach can contribute value when aligned to shared goals, such as student engagement or mastery of standards.

  For example, in a middle school team meeting, a science teacher who emphasizes hands-on experimentation and an ELA teacher who prefers direct instruction might initially clash over how to support literacy across content areas. By focusing on the shared goal—helping students strengthen academic vocabulary—the team can blend both perspectives: using inquiry-driven lab reports that also reinforce explicit writing skills. In this way, teachers honor one another's professional expertise, reduce tension, and transform differing viewpoints into opportunities for collaboration rather than competition.

- **Refer to data.** Anchoring disagreements in data makes the conversation more objective, focusing on evidence rather than personal preference. Again, using student work examples helps with this. In addition to formative and summative assessment, consider incorporating computer program usage reports, peer observation results, and other relevant data points.
- **Revisit the relationship.** If repeated conflicts occur, proactively resetting or revisiting the relationship offers an opportunity to rebuild trust and move forward productively. Say, "We've had several challenging discussions in the past couple of weeks. I just wanted to check in and ensure our relationship is OK." This prompt might be one way to start such a conversation.

Feeling unsteady with any of these tactics is normal; the teacher may consider rehearsing or role-playing challenging conversations in a low-stakes environment. Experimenting with tone, body language, and strategic pauses and practicing with a friend or trusted colleague can reduce tension. In addition, a teacher might consider formal training in active listening and reflective mirroring, inspired by global peace-building methodologies. These approaches can defuse misunderstandings, preserve emotional well-being, and cultivate a climate of mutual respect even under stressful circumstances (Neff, 2023).

Reignite PLCs

Judith Warren Little (1993) provided influential early research in teacher collaboration and collegial work cultures, laying the necessary groundwork for what would later be called professional learning communities. In the 1980s and early '90s, her research highlighted the significance of teacher relationships, shared practices, and a focus on collective improvement—core ideas that are now central to PLCs. Considering these earliest notions of collaboration, consider how PLCs might be leveraged to promote collegial self-care and well-being. Consider the following approaches:

- PLCs can move beyond standard textbook or data analysis by exploring interdisciplinary projects or delving into cutting-edge research on the neuroscience of education, social-emotional learning, or globally sustainable education. Encouraging members to bring unconventional resources, such as studies on physical activity's impact on cognitive performance or articles on culturally responsive teaching, expands the scope of professional growth (Ratey & Manning, 2018).

- To enhance self-care, PLCs might dedicate a portion of each meeting to "well-being rounds" where members share recent successes in managing their workloads or highlight a new technique for stress reduction. Over time, these positive exchanges foster an environment in which professional growth and personal well-being are equally valued, creating a more holistic approach to ongoing teacher development (Aguilar, 2018).

- Reflection need not be solitary. Teachers can engage in collective reflection, where they work in small groups to temporarily step outside the school environment—perhaps into a local park or quiet cultural center—to evaluate teaching practices and emotional well-being. Guided by prompts inspired by research on reflective practitioners, participants can celebrate growth, acknowledge stress triggers, and reimagine their teaching roles through a more supportive lens (Schön, 1983).

- Enhance team planning meetings by adding a creativity station where participants experiment with new teaching modalities, such as storyline-based math problems or culturally relevant arts integration, before finalizing lesson plans. This station can hold tactile resources, digital tools, or physical objects that spark unconventional thinking. Collaborative planning becomes a creative laboratory that breaks monotony and distributes workload evenly among colleagues (Csikszentmihalyi, 2013).

- Reinforce a sense of shared accomplishment by celebrating small wins, such as successfully piloting a student-led lesson. Over time, these sessions become a source of emotional fuel as educators feel less isolated in lesson creation and more united in overcoming common challenges. Ultimately, collaborative planning shares resources and nurtures collective resilience against burnout.

- Focus on what worked. A common shortfall in many PLCs is the lack of meaningful discussion about which teaching strategies were successful and why (Young et al., 2023). During data analysis, teachers often overlook—or only briefly mention—the approaches that led to student improvement, even if those gains came from just one or two teachers. In most cases, these successful teachers are not doing anything extraordinary; they may simply be providing a few more practice opportunities or conducting more small-group reteaching sessions, and such subtle changes in instruction are powerful and can be adopted by everyone. Without thoroughly examining what went well and why, these practical strategies get lost as attention shifts to areas in which students did not do as well. To be clear, we are not suggesting that teams ignore student learning gaps revealed by formative assessment. Instead, we recommend spending more time investigating the practices of teachers who experienced even modest success so those practices can inform and improve everyone's instruction.

• Two examples illustrate how teachers reshaped their PLCs. In North Carolina, a group of elementary teachers formed a study group focused on improving instruction. With a suggested text and minimal guidance from a coach, they structured their meetings like a book club, meeting weekly for one hour to discuss the reading and its practical applications. As a result, they reported feeling more motivated, less stressed (despite being in a low-performing school), and proud of their professional growth. In the suburbs of Chicago, Illinois, two educators organized a weekly summer series in one teacher's backyard to address a pressing issue: supporting students who have experienced trauma. They invited a relative who was a trained social worker to guide the discussions. Both of these teacher-led, small-group initiatives reduced stress and enhanced professional skills, echoing Judith Warren Little's foundational findings that collegial, small-group collaboration among teachers fuels meaningful professional growth. In both cases, the teacher groups noted striking increases in their students' subsequent academic gains—a testament to the finding from Hattie's work that productive collaboration leads to one of the highest impacts on student academic achievement: collective teacher efficacy (effect size = 1.01; Hattie, 2024).

Long-Term, High-Prep Strategies

Use Buddy Systems

Buddy systems evolve beyond casual pairings when they incorporate structured yet flexible protocols for emotional support. Colleagues might schedule brief wellness check-ins over coffee or on short daily walks, ensuring there is always a trusted partner who can listen without judgment. Incorporating a digital platform where buddies track their moods or share encouraging messages adds another layer of support (Hwang et al., 2020).

Conduct a Book Study

Gathering some friends to conduct a little "read and discuss" enlivens collegiality and promotes self-care. Here are some books that teachers commonly recommend for these book studies:

- *The Body Keeps the Score: Brain, Mind, and Body in the Healing of Trauma* (2014) by Van der Kolk
- *Burnout: The Secret to Unlocking the Stress Cycle* (2019) by Nagoski and Nagoski
- *Culturally Responsive Self-Care Practices for Early Childhood Educators* (2019) by Nicholson, Shimpi Driscoll, Kurtz, Márquez, and Wesley
- *Onward: Cultivating Emotional Resilience in Educators* (2018) by Aguilar

Sustaining excellent teaching requires sustaining the teacher. The most effective educators recognize that caring for themselves is not indulgent—it's instructional. Every act of self-awareness, reflection, or collaboration strengthens both personal well-being and classroom impact. By building supportive alliances, setting healthy boundaries, and embracing practical wellness routines, teachers model resilience for their students and colleagues alike. When educators protect their own energy and purpose, they create classrooms that thrive on balance, empathy, and joy—conditions where both teachers and learners can flourish.

9

Cultural Competency, Inclusivity, and Equity

Long-Term, High-Prep Strategies

Most teachers want their classrooms to be places where students feel recognized, respected, and supported. However, building that kind of environment doesn't come automatically; it requires purposeful choices and a willingness to reflect and adjust as the lesson progresses. This chapter provides practical, realistic strategies for making classrooms inclusive and equitable places, from thoughtfully designed professional development programs to incorporating books that reflect students' lived experiences and engaging families and communities as meaningful educational partners.

The work described in this chapter is a fundamental commitment for most educators and makes teaching and learning richer, more joyful, and reflective of the diverse, interconnected world beyond the classroom walls. Explore more than 80 equity-driven techniques that ensure every voice is valued and every perspective enriches classroom life. The strategies here are organized in three categories based on the level of effort and preparation required for implementation:

- Immediate, Low-Prep Strategies
- Routine, Moderate-Prep Strategies
- Long-Term, High-Prep Strategies

Immediate, Low-Prep Strategies

Implement Pronoun Awareness Activities

Respectful pronoun use supports a culture of inclusivity. Small, everyday classroom practices—such as asking students to share their pronouns during introductions, using posters that show a range of pronouns, or role-playing respectful conversations—can go a long way to help all students feel seen. Teachers can also fold these conversations into lessons they're already teaching, like exploring pronouns in a grammar unit or discussing identity while reading literature. When these efforts are consistent and woven into everyday routines, they help create a classroom in which students feel safe, respected, and free to be themselves (Ryan & Hermann-Wilmarth, 2022).

Celebrate Multicultural Events

Bringing multicultural celebrations into the classroom sparks real excitement among students. It's important to emphasize that this is more than checking off holidays or decorating with flags and posters—though those things can be a fun start. What really makes a difference is the way students begin to lean in, ask questions, and show genuine interest in one another's traditions. They might try a dish they've never tasted before or light up while telling the class about a family celebration. These small but meaningful moments— sharing a story, explaining a custom, hearing about a new holiday— help students feel proud of who they are and eager to learn about the people around them. That's the kind of classroom community most teachers want to develop: one where diversity isn't just taught from a textbook but felt daily (Nieto, 2022).

A school where Keith, Judith, and Angela worked in Arizona celebrates Día de los Muertos (Day of the Dead), a Mexican tradition, by creating altars (*ofrendas*) and learning about the history and cultural significance of the holiday. Events such as this give students a chance to celebrate their roots, learn about their classmates' traditions, and take pride in their cultural backgrounds. They also create a more welcoming environment in which different perspectives are respected and valued. When everyone takes part, students walk away with a deeper appreciation for the customs and stories that shape their classmates' lives—and a better understanding of why representation and cultural awareness matter in school.

Create Safe Spaces for Identity Exploration

Offering opportunities for students to dive into projects about their identities can lead to some eye-opening classroom moments. For instance, elementary kids might assemble shoebox dioramas that show important traditions from home, such as Sunday dinners or holiday celebrations. Middle schoolers could create podcasts where they interview family members about their heritage, recording stories that classmates get to listen to when exploring their heritage. High school students might write personal narratives or poems reflecting their experiences growing up between two cultures or navigating their unique identities in creative writing. When students see their classmates sharing real, personal stories, walls tend to come down, and conversations start happening naturally. These authentic projects help kids realize they're not alone in their experiences and show them how powerful and fascinating diversity can be (Nieto, 2022).

Establish Student Voice Panels

Student voice panels let kids comfortably talk about their own experiences, including how they see themselves, what it's like fitting in, or their everyday lives at school. When teachers clearly set the tone for kindness and let students choose if they want to join in, it leads to real, meaningful conversations. When students have a chance to share their stories, it helps their classmates truly understand where they're coming from—and it shows them that every voice counts. Whether through structured discussions or informal chats, making space for student perspectives builds connection, keeps kids engaged, and helps create a classroom that feels open and respectful. Over time, students come to see that their ideas and experiences aren't just welcome—they're an important part of shaping a diverse and thoughtful community (Sensoy & DiAngelo, 2022).

Use Inclusive Language for People with Disabilities

Using inclusive language is essential for respecting the dignity and individuality of people with disabilities. The American Psychological Association (APA) recommends using inclusive, bias-free language to support equity, respect, and dignity for all. Figure 9.1 presents a simplified chart highlighting key suggestions from the APA's Inclusive Language Guidelines for referring to individuals with disabilities.

Figure 9.1   Simplified Inclusive Language Guidelines

Avoid Saying	Say This Instead	Rationale
Disabled or *handicapped*	*People with disabilities*	Person-first language centers on the individual, not the disability.
Autistic person	*A person with autism* (unless otherwise preferred)	APA recommends person-first unless the individual prefers identity-first.
Suffering from or *afflicted with*	*Has* or *Lives with* [condition]	This avoids negative or pitying language.
Wheelchair-bound	*A person who uses a wheelchair*	This describes mobility-aid use rather than implying restriction.
Mentally ill or *insane*	*A person with a mental health condition*	This reduces the stigma around mental health.
Crippled or *lame*	*A person with a mobility disability*	This uses respectful, specific language.
Normal person	*A person without a disability*	This avoids implying that people with disabilities are abnormal.

Source: Adapted from *Inclusive Language Guidelines* by the American Psychological Association (2025). https://www.apa.org/about/apa/equity-diversity-inclusion/language-guidelines

Routine, Moderate-Prep Strategies

Organize Community Engagement

Classrooms flourish when educators proactively build meaningful partnerships with the local community. Inviting community members—such as local artists, authors, business owners, parents, elders, and cultural leaders—to share their lived experiences and cultural knowledge significantly enhances student learning and engagement. Imagine inviting a local chef to class to show students how to cook a dish that reflects their culture, or welcoming elders to share stories and traditions passed down for generations. These experiences help students connect with the history and richness of their community in ways a textbook simply can't. They also give students an honest look into cultural traditions and ways of life, bringing learning to life in a way that's hard to match.

When schools invite the community in, it opens the door for students to better understand the world and view differences with curiosity, empathy, and a sense of respect (Yosso & Solórzano, 2022). It also sends a strong message to students who don't often see their backgrounds represented in school materials. When their families, neighbors, or cultural leaders are welcomed into the classroom, it tells students who they are—and where they come from—matters. These moments help students feel more connected, seen, and valued at school. At the same time, they strengthen the school's relationship with the broader community. Events such as cultural nights, career panels with diverse professionals, or neighborhood service projects help create a learning environment grounded in real life, making school more engaging for everyone involved.

Ultimately, sustained community engagement enriches the educational landscape, making classrooms vibrant, inclusive, and culturally responsive spaces where all students can thrive. A high school in southern Arizona, which has a 98 percent Hispanic population, holds a yearly college and career fair. They make it a point to invite former students back to speak with 9th and 10th graders about what comes next—whether it's preparing for college, exploring careers, or adjusting to life after graduation. There's real power in hearing from someone who once walked the same halls, faced similar struggles, and found their own path forward.

When students connect with someone whose journey reflects their own, dreams such as college or a future career start to feel less out of reach. It stops being a far-off idea and becomes something they can picture for themselves. Seeing someone who looks like them, shares their background, or has overcome similar challenges sends a powerful message: *you belong here*. It challenges stereotypes and reinforces that their goals are valid and possible. Sometimes, just one honest conversation with someone who's been there can build confidence, ignite motivation, and help a student take that next step forward.

Develop Professional Development Programs

Just as students need consistent learning experiences, educators require regular opportunities to advance their skills, particularly in equity and inclusion. Effective professional development is essential to establish equitable classrooms because educators who are proficient in culturally responsive practices can more effectively engage all learners. Take a school that sets aside time each month for staff to grow their cultural awareness. In one session, teachers might talk through ways to connect more deeply with immigrant families. In another, they could swap ideas for running literature circles where every student feels included and heard. These professional learning programs should be ongoing rather than single events, collaborative in nature, and directly applicable to classroom practice (Young & Osborne, 2023).

Organize Bias Awareness Workshops

Recognizing and addressing personal biases is crucial for equitable education. We all absorb stereotypes or assumptions from society—often unconsciously—that can unintentionally shape our expectations or interactions with students. Workshops dedicated to bias awareness help educators uncover and actively counteract these unconscious prejudices, creating a classroom atmosphere of understanding and equality (Sue & Sue, 2023). In a bias awareness workshop, teachers might participate in an implicit association test to reveal hidden biases or examine scenarios involving microaggressions in school settings. For instance, an educator might discover they frequently mispronounce or shorten students' names from particular cultures or realize they unconsciously discipline boys and girls differently. By illuminating such patterns in a supportive and nonjudgmental environment, teachers can initiate meaningful change in their daily interactions with students.

These workshops also introduce practical strategies for managing biases, such as mindful pauses—brief moments teachers take to check their positive or negative assumptions about a student before responding to behavior or grading assignments. Another helpful approach involves perspective-taking exercises, where educators reflect on how a scenario might be perceived differently by a student or family from another background. Research shows that unchecked bias can have real classroom consequences. For instance, studies have found that teachers sometimes underestimate the academic potential or behavioral intent of Black boys and multilingual learners compared with their peers, even when performance levels are similar (Gilliam et al., 2016; Okonfua & Eberhardt, 2015).

In education, similar biased assumptions—such as underestimating a bilingual student's abilities based solely on their accent—can severely limit opportunities for success. Working on internal biases significantly improves teacher expectations and estimates of student achievement, which is a decisive factor in student academic outcomes (effect size = 1.30; Hattie, 2023). Little by little, schools can build a culture in which teachers feel comfortable holding one another accountable in kind, respectful ways. A colleague might say, "I've noticed that some of the students of color or those with bigger behavior challenges are often seated in the back. Do you want to brainstorm how we could switch that up so everyone feels more included?" When educators take the time to notice patterns and challenge their own assumptions, it creates a more supportive, fair learning environment for all students (Sue & Sue, 2023).

It is imperative that educators are aware of the biases, stereotypes, and missing stories of the marginalized populations they teach. This point could not be more painfully illustrated than by the following story we heard from a parent. A mother shared a moment with her 1st grader, Charlie, after school one afternoon. He was excited to tell her everything he'd learned about Native Americans and said, "They lived in teepees. They hunted buffalo. They had really simple lives."

The mother listened closely, then softly asked, "Charlie, where do Native Americans live today?"

He thought for a moment before answering confidently, "They don't live anywhere now. Native Americans were from way back. They're not around anymore."

The mom took a slow breath, letting that answer settle. Then, without a word, she turned the car down a street Charlie knew well. He looked up and asked, "Where are we going?"

She smiled and answered, "We're going to visit Aunt Gwynn. She's from the San Felipe Pueblo, and I think she'll show you that Native Americans are very much alive and well today."

Charlie seemed puzzled. "But Aunt Gwynn lives in a real house, not a teepee!" he said. "How can she be Native American?"

"Exactly," the mom replied, nodding. "That's exactly why we're going to see her."

Promote Gender Equality

Regularly bringing up gender equality in class helps chip away at outdated stereotypes, but it has to go beyond lectures and slides. Take the well-known classroom activity where students are asked to draw or describe a scientist, a surgeon, or an engineer. Studies such as the Draw-a-Scientist test (www.nsta.org/draw-scientist) reveal that many students, especially as they get older, tend to picture men in these roles without even thinking about it. Teachers can incorporate this activity into their lessons as a starting point for honest, eye-opening discussions. After students finish their drawings, teachers can follow up with videos or stories that spotlight women breaking barriers—female astronauts, surgeons, or tech leaders, for example.

These moments prompt students to pause and think about their assumptions, opening the door for honest conversations about gender and fairness. Helping kids recognize these patterns early on builds a classroom in which inclusion and respect are the norm and where students feel empowered to push back against stereotypes (Butler, 2022). Even though the 2024 Olympics made history by reaching equal representation between men and women (International Olympic Committee, 2024), that kind of balance isn't always easy to find on the school playground. During recess, boys often dominate the space with organized or pick-up games of football, basketball, or soccer. Meanwhile, girls are frequently left out or choose not to participate. To create a more balanced and welcoming environment, some schools have started organizing team sports by classroom or using other inclusive setups that move away from dividing kids by gender.

Elevate Disability Inclusion and Awareness

Inclusive classrooms make space for all kinds of learners and openly teach students that having a disability is just one of many ways people can be unique. The use of visual supports, audiobooks, or sensory-friendly materials—part of what's called Universal Design for Learning (UDL)—helps every student succeed. Teachers can also normalize talking about disabilities by sharing stories, chatting openly, focusing on what students do well, and helping classmates support one another. Introducing disability history and advocacy in lessons helps students appreciate diversity, and it fosters empathy and creates an inclusive classroom community that respects and celebrates differences (Nieto, 2022).

A special education teacher whom Tamarra observed took a proactive and empowering approach to promoting inclusion in her elementary classroom. During the first week of school, she worked with her students who had disabilities to create short presentations explaining their conditions in ways classmates could easily understand. Whether a student had autism, Down syndrome, or another learning difference, she sat with them and helped them share what they were good at, what was challenging, and how they learned best. They used pictures, easy-to-understand words, and playful activities to keep their classmates engaged. After each presentation, she encouraged classmates to ask thoughtful, respectful questions. This set a tone where students felt safe sharing and learning from one another. It also gave students with disabilities a stronger sense of voice and confidence, while helping the whole class build empathy and mutual respect from day one.

In addition to the student-led presentations, the teacher also took the lead in planning schoolwide sessions to build awareness around autism and Down syndrome. She used a mix of videos, personal stories, and open conversations to help students understand that people learn and grow in different ways. Through these efforts, she helped her students view disabilities not as something unusual or intimidating but as one of the many ways people can be unique. As time went on, these activities helped create a classroom in which kindness, patience, and understanding came naturally. Her thoughtful approach didn't just shift attitudes—it reduced bullying, opened the door to real friendships, and laid the groundwork for a more inclusive school where every student felt like they belonged.

Foster Cross-Cultural Peer Groups

Teachers can create opportunities for students to learn more about one another by setting up activities that encourage cultural sharing. These kinds of experiences help build empathy and reduce misunderstandings. For instance, small-group discussions or classroom events where students talk about their family traditions or personal stories can spark curiosity and foster a deeper appreciation for the diverse backgrounds in the room. This helps everyone in the class learn from one another and appreciate their differences. Involving students as "experts" of their own cultures empowers them, deepens mutual understanding, and helps break down self-segregation. The power of well-crafted classroom discussions on academic student achievement cannot be overstated (effect size = 0.82; Hattie, 2024). Teachers can help students talk respectfully with one another, show them how to use welcoming language, and switch up group members often so everyone gets to know different classmates. Doing this regularly helps build friendships across cultures and creates a more caring and connected classroom (Nieto, 2022).

Build an Inclusive Classroom Library

Books can open hearts and shift perspectives in ways few other tools can. Building an inclusive classroom library, with both physical and electronic books, means thoughtfully choosing stories that reflect a wide range of cultures, identities, and lived experiences.

When students see themselves in the pages—and meet characters whose lives are very different—it builds both self-worth and understanding. Teachers can fill their shelves with a mix of novels, picture books, biographies, and poetry written by diverse authors and centered on diverse voices (Thomas, 2022). Consider stories that include different races and ethnicities, various family structures, characters with disabilities, books set in non-Western countries, and stories that explore gender identity or immigration.

For example, an elementary teacher might include picture books like *Julian Is a Mermaid* (celebrating gender expression) or *Thunder Boy Jr.* (featuring a Native American family) alongside classics. A middle school teacher could add novels like *The First Rule of Punk* (about a Mexican American girl finding her voice) or *Inside Out & Back Again* (about a Vietnamese refugee family). When introducing these books, frame them as part of learning. Say, "Our library has voices from all over the world and from many different perspectives. Let's explore them." You can also highlight a book of the week from the library related to a current event or topic in your curriculum, bridging diverse texts and daily lessons.

Inviting student input is also powerful. Asking students what cultures or issues they wish were represented or involving them in choosing new books is a great approach. If you have students from, say, Somalia or Haiti, adding a folktale or story from those cultures can make those students beam with pride, and their classmates get to learn from a peer expert. It's important to note that an inclusive library should avoid stereotypes. For instance, ensure books portray people of different backgrounds in roles beyond historical hardships (i.e., not just stories of slavery or immigration struggles but also joy, innovation, and everyday life). Maintaining such a library is an ongoing process. Rotate books throughout the year, tie selections to heritage months without limiting them to those times, and continue seeking out new titles (school librarians and resources such as the

We Need Diverse Books movement are great resources). The impact of this effort is profound. When each student can find a story where they feel seen, it validates their identity; when they read about others unlike themselves, it humanizes those differences. Over time, inclusive classroom libraries produce empathetic and curious readers about the world.

Implement Inclusive Lesson Planning

Creating inclusive lesson plans means making sure diverse voices and experiences are part of everyday teaching—not something added in once in a while. Instead of treating diversity as a separate topic, teachers can build it right into their learning goals. That might look like highlighting inventors of all races and genders in a science unit or choosing books by authors of color and stories from different cultures when planning a literature unit (Gay, 2022). The goal is to make lessons more relevant and reflective of the world students live in, and it all starts with a simple shift in mindset: thinking intentionally about whose stories are being told—and whose are missing.

A guiding question for lessons is "Whose voices are present here, and whose might be missing?" If the topic is the American Revolution, for example, incorporating the perspectives of Native Americans or enslaved people during that era increases the voices present. In an elementary science lesson about space, astronauts such as Mae Jemison (the first Black woman in space) or Kalpana Chawla (an Indian American astronaut) should be highlighted to show that science is for everyone. It's also about connecting to students' lives. Minor tweaks in examples and visuals can make a big difference. A math teacher could use culturally relevant word problems (for instance, using names and contexts that reflect the cultures in the class or framing a statistics lesson around demographic data from students' communities). An inclusive kindergarten lesson on family could acknowledge that families come in many forms; some have a mom and dad, some have a single parent, some have two moms or two dads, some live with grandparents, and all are to be respected.

While planning, the teacher can use a diversity checklist that includes "Does this lesson include a diverse example or context? Have I avoided one-sided narratives or generalizations? Are materials (stories, case studies, images) coming from a variety of sources?" Over the course of a unit or semester, aim for balance so that no single culture or perspective dominates. Inclusive lesson planning also involves varying your teaching methods to honor different ways of learning—another nod to equity. For example, teachers can mix things up by using group discussions, quiet reflection time, visuals, music, or movement—approaches that may connect with a variety of cultural ways of learning and communicating.

Another powerful move is to invite students into the planning process. Let them choose topics for projects or research that reflect their interests or cultural backgrounds. When lessons are built this way, it sends a clear message: Every student is capable, and every student's identity adds value to the learning experience. Over time, students will see the curriculum as a mirror reflecting the value of their own identity and a window into the lives of others, which is a hallmark of an equitable education.

Conduct Equity Audits

Just like teachers check in on student learning with assessments, they can also take a closer look at their classrooms to see how inclusive and equitable their practices really are. One way to do this is by conducting regular equity audits. The teacher takes stock of things like who speaks up most in class, which students are getting redirected or disciplined, and how diverse the materials on the shelves really are. This is a way to catch patterns we might not otherwise notice and make sure our good intentions are actually leading to fair and supportive experiences for all students (Khalifa, 2023).

For example, a teacher might keep a simple tally during class discussions to see if they are inadvertently calling on certain students (say, the more outspoken or those from particular backgrounds) more than others. The results might reveal that English language learners or quieter students speak up far less frequently. Once that information is gathered, the teacher can make thoughtful changes—such as using specific strategies—to ensure every student has a chance to contribute. Another part of an equity audit might involve looking at grades or who's getting access to advanced classes and special opportunities. If students from certain racial groups or with disabilities are noticeably underrepresented, it's worth digging into the reasons. From there, steps can be taken—like offering more support or personally encouraging those students to take part—to open the door a little wider for everyone.

An equity audit can also include a review of the physical environment and curriculum. Do the posters, books, and historical figures highlighted reflect diverse genders, cultures, and abilities, or are some perspectives missing? A checklist might be used where the teacher inventories the classroom library or wall displays for representation. Teachers can continually refine their approach by treating the classroom as a work in progress and using equity audits like a scientist uses experiments. The process doesn't have to be complicated; it can be as simple as jotting down personal reflections or as structured as a teamwide review of student data.

What matters most is a willingness to take a clear, honest look at what's working and where things could be more equitable. When an issue is identified, such as a particular group lagging in science achievement, the teacher (with support from colleagues or coaches) can help devise solutions—maybe incorporating culturally relevant examples in science lessons or mentoring targeted students. Over time, these audits and adjustments promote lasting equity by ensuring that no subset of students is overlooked.

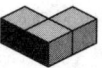

Long-Term, High-Prep Strategies

Lead Professional Development

Just as students need consistent learning experiences, educators require regular opportunities to advance their skills, particularly in equity and inclusion. Effective professional development is essential to establishing equitable classrooms because educators who are proficient in culturally responsive practices can more effectively engage all learners. Imagine a school that sets aside time each month for staff to grow their cultural awareness. In one session, teachers might talk through ways to connect more deeply with immigrant families. In another, they could swap ideas for running literature circles where every student feels included and heard. These professional learning programs should be ongoing rather than single events, collaborative in nature, and directly applicable to classroom practice (Young & Osborne, 2023).

According to Hattie's visible learning research (2023), professional development designed explicitly around student learning substantially and positively affects student academic outcomes (effect size = 0.44). To maximize this impact, teachers might engage in practical activities such as engaging in role-playing scenarios involving bias, analyzing case studies, reflecting on personal classroom challenges, and sharing effective strategies from their experiences as teachers—or even their students' memories. School leaders can support this work by carving out time and resources to make it happen. That might involve hosting on-site workshops, bringing in guest speakers, or covering costs for teachers to attend conferences focused on equity and inclusion. As Darling-Hammond and Hyler (2023) point out, these kinds of ongoing, hands-on experiences give teachers the confidence and skills to create classrooms in which all students feel like they belong. Treating cultural competency as a continually evolving skill tied to student achievement—akin to the ongoing professional learning required in other fields—clearly signals to educators that inclusive teaching is a prioritized, fundamental component of their role.

Angela was once observing classrooms in a school, and as she talked with a teacher afterward, she asked about two students who did not engage in the learning during the lesson. The teacher broke down in tears and said, "They don't speak English, and I don't speak their language. I have no training in how to teach language learners. I go home at night and have a knot in my stomach because I just let them sit there and not learn every day." Together, she and Angela researched what her district had to offer for training. They involved the instructional coach and department chair for multilingual learners. The teacher received materials and co-teaching training. As a result, the students became engaged in the learning. Remember, it's always OK to say, "I don't know how to do that." Seeking out others who do know puts you in a position of strength.

Develop an Inclusive Curriculum

Beyond individual lessons, curricula should reflect and celebrate student diversity. Developing an inclusive curriculum means carefully looking at what's taught across different grades and subjects, then purposefully including diverse viewpoints, stories, and historical contributions throughout the lessons (Gay, 2022). This work often requires collaboration at the department or school level, but individual teachers can also initiate change by auditing their curricula and making incremental adjustments. For instance, a high school English department could revise their reading lists so at least half the literature comes from authors of diverse ethnic and cultural backgrounds rather than including a token novel by an author of color. Similarly, a history teacher might organize their year's units to reflect significant historical events from diverse geographic regions—including European, North American, Latin American, African, Middle Eastern, Asian, and Indigenous perspectives—and highlight the contributions of historically marginalized groups such as women and working-class individuals.

Diversity shouldn't be something that only shows up during specific months or at special events. It works best when it's part of everyday teaching. In social studies, for instance, themes like "Migration and Movement" naturally lend themselves to exploring a range of voices and experiences. Students might study westward expansion but also learn about the great migration of African Americans, immigration stories from Asia and Latin America, or what life is like for refugees in the world today. These perspectives add depth and meaning to the learning. Teachers can make lessons even more meaningful by connecting them directly to students' own backgrounds. For instance, in a science class studying plants, students could share how their families traditionally use certain herbs or plants.

It's also helpful for teachers to team up with colleagues and community members—maybe inviting a local historian or elder to class—to help make sure lessons are accurate, respectful, and reflective of different cultural viewpoints. Creating an inclusive curriculum isn't something to check off once and move on; it's an ongoing process. As classrooms shift and the world changes, lessons need to keep evolving, too. When students see their own lives and identities reflected in what they're learning, they're more likely to stay engaged and curious. It also helps them connect with new ideas, understand different perspectives, and feel more prepared to thrive in a diverse world.

Building an inclusive curriculum is fundamentally about equity and ensuring education honors every student and community served. Inclusive practices such as these help every student find themselves in the "business" of the classroom. When thinking about a sheet of printed text, it is clear there are margins on all four sides. The "business" of the writing lies within those margins. When students don't find themselves "within the margins," they sometimes escape into the blank space and mentally opt out of the learning. In short, they become marginalized—not because they don't want to learn but because they can't find a way to enter the classroom business. Inclusive practices bring students in from the margins.

Encourage Identity Projects and Flexible Expression

Flexible identity projects let students explore and proudly share their backgrounds in ways they're most comfortable with, such as art, writing, presentations, or even digital media. Teachers can encourage students to dive deeper than just ethnicity; they can share hobbies, local traditions, or special family customs. Students must have clear guidance at every step. The teacher should encourage everyone to listen thoughtfully and respectfully when classmates share their stories. This kind of environment encourages students to take pride in who they are, brings classmates closer together, and creates a space where everyone feels valued and safe being themselves (Nieto, 2022).

Cultural competency is not an extra initiative; it's the daily practice of teaching with empathy, curiosity, and respect. By intentionally reflecting on bias, celebrating diversity, and embedding multiple perspectives into lessons, educators expand students' capacity for understanding both themselves and others. Each classroom that values every learner's story becomes a small model of the inclusive world we hope students will help create. When teachers commit to this ongoing work—listening, learning, and adjusting—they transform equity from a goal into a living part of instructional excellence.

10

Take Action

This chapter provides little hacks for the implementation of what has been learned reading this book. Discovering a great idea from this book, a friend, or a personal innovation is one thing, but sometimes, it's quite a leap to implement that idea entirely. This culminating chapter distills 40 quick-implementation hacks for sustaining growth and lasting professional momentum. We've structured this chapter's strategies into three groups, each reflecting a different degree of preparation and complexity:

- Immediate, Low-Prep Strategies
- Routine, Moderate-Prep Strategies
- Long-Term, High-Prep Strategies

Immediate, Low-Prep Strategies

Start Small

When trying out a new strategy in teaching, it's helpful to start small to avoid getting frustrated. If students need to work on asking deeper questions, consider tossing in one or two thoughtful, open-ended questions per lesson. Once doing that regularly becomes comfortable, higher-level questions can be gradually added more often and in different parts of the lessons. Think of this like learning to play an instrument. You wouldn't try to master a concerto in one sitting but would start with a few measures and build from there.

Use Technology Aids

Harness technology as a personal assistant for professional growth. Digital tools can do more than send reminders; they can help track habits, visualize progress, and celebrate small wins along the way. Apps like Habitica, Todoist, or Streaks allow teachers to gamify professional routines by assigning points or badges for completing tasks such as "ask for student reflections" or "use a wait-time pause." For teachers who prefer simplicity, a recurring reminder on a smartwatch or phone can serve as a quick digital nudge before class begins: "Try a formative question today" or "End the lesson with a reflection prompt."

Beyond reminders, habit-tracking dashboards or journaling apps (like Notion, Google Keep, or Daylio) can help teachers document progress over time, turning abstract goals into visible data. Tracking practice of a new questioning technique five times over the course of a week provides tangible reinforcement and motivation. For collaborative environments, shared digital planners or team apps like Trello, Slack, or Microsoft Teams make it easy to align new habits across grade-level or subject teams, keeping collective commitments visible and accountable.

When used intentionally, technology aids serve as an invisible coaching partner. They help automate the accountability that new professional habits require, freeing teachers to focus on what truly matters—student learning. The goal isn't to add one more task but to use digital tools as quiet, consistent reminders that keep growth work visible, manageable, and, most importantly, sustainable.

Change Settings to Reflect

Stepping out of a usual environment to reflect on progress can help the process. For example, take a journal or lesson plan book to a coffee shop or sit outside during a planning period. Switching up surroundings can inspire creativity and reduce mental blocks that sometimes accompany routine settings. Instead of always sitting at a desk for lunch, a quick walk around the school track can provide a change of pace and perspective.

Normalize Mistakes in Your Practice

Keep in mind that making mistakes is a completely normal—and even helpful—part of growing as a teacher, no matter how experienced a teacher is. If a new strategy doesn't go as smoothly as hoped, a thoughtful pause to consider what happened and how it could be tweaked may make it work better next time. For instance, if a planned group activity doesn't engage students effectively, consider adjustments such as providing clearer, more explicit instructions or breaking students into smaller, more manageable groups. (As a side note, in our fairly extensive experience, we find student groups of no more than three to be the ideal; that way, everyone has a clear task and it's easier to keep all students accountable.) Teaching mistakes are akin to failed recipes; they offer up insight into potential pitfalls and guide the teacher toward better instructional outcomes. Embracing mistakes openly in the classroom can help model for students how to build up some resilience and a growth mindset, reinforcing the message that learning often involves trial and error (Dweck, 2016).

Reframe Critical Feedback

Critical feedback can easily spark stress or self-doubt, but it doesn't have to. One way to reduce that emotional weight is to treat feedback less like a personal critique and more like a practical to-do list. When a coach, colleague, or supervisor shares suggestions, the teacher should focus on the specific actions that can be taken right away. For example, if they suggest classroom transitions need improvement, strategies such as adding a visual timer or incorporating a consistent phrase into the lesson can be considered. When receiving feedback, the teacher can also take control of the conversation by asking clarifying questions about how to implement suggestions. This keeps the focus on improvement, not evaluation. Breaking things into small, manageable steps makes the process feel more approachable—much like organizing one drawer at a time instead of overhauling an entire room. The key is shifting from reacting emotionally to responding strategically.

Routine, Moderate-Prep Strategies

Annotate New Habits in Lesson Plans

Even if plans are kept short and simple, include new teaching practices in lesson outlines to help make them a regular part of the daily teaching routine. For example, if the change desired is to encourage student discussion, write down specific moments in the lesson where there can be a planned pause and invite questions or peer interaction. Consider which students will be asked to respond, how much time the discussion will take, and what backup questions are planned if the first ones don't generate discussion. Explicit planning ensures intentionality of the new habit, increasing the likelihood of consistent implementation. In short, the teacher sets a clear road map for success by embedding habits into lesson plans.

When trying out a new teaching strategy, a triple-column lesson plan can help keep the lesson clear and focused (Young et al., 2023). This format builds on Lemov's (2021) two-column idea—where one column outlines what the teacher does and the other shows what students do—by adding a third column for reminders and cues to support the new technique. Figure 10.1 turns this planning concept into a concrete visual tool. It shows how a triple-column lesson plan helps teachers intentionally map what *they* do, what *students* do, and when to apply reminders or cues that reinforce a new instructional habit. By laying out teacher actions, student responses, and targeted strategies side-by-side, the design makes invisible planning decisions visible on paper. This structure not only clarifies each phase of the lesson but also ensures that emerging habits—such as equitable

Figure 10.1   Triple-Column Lesson Design

Teacher Actions	Student Actions	**Targeted Skill or Strategy** *(The example here is "ensuring students stay academically engaged.")*
Post the activator or warm-up.	Students write responses in their notebooks.	The teacher moves among the class, taking roll while ensuring all students write.
State the lesson objective and rationale.	Students chorally repeat the objective.	Scan the room, looking for everyone to speak. Repeat the process once or twice if needed.
Demonstrate the first problem.	Students copy the teacher's model.	Tell students to write. Scan the room to see who is writing and who is not.
Practice 4-6 problems: rotating teacher leading and students leading the problem steps. Stop and check everyone's steps along the way. Combine more of the problem steps in each new example.	Students complete problems step by step with the entire class. Students check each other's work and discuss errors they made and how to correct them in the following problem.	Pace the room to ensure everyone completes all steps for all problems. Focus on *what to do*, not *what not to do*. For example, instead of "Archie, you're not working," say, "Archie, complete step 2 now," or "Archie, pick up your pencil."

The lesson follows a similar pattern through lesson closure, focusing on teacher activities, student activities, and actions the teacher takes to maintain student engagement.

Source: Adapted from *The Instructional Coaching Handbook* (p. 181), by A. K. Young, A. B. Julien, and T. Osborne, 2023, ASCD.

participation or consistent feedback—are embedded directly into the daily routine. In short, this framework transforms intention into implementation, helping teachers see exactly where and how their new practice lives within the flow of instruction.

Set Explicit Goals with Milestones

Set a measurable 30-day goal for the new habit and break it into weekly objectives. For example, if the aim is to use more structured formative assessment, the teacher's first milestone could be incorporating it into one lesson during the first week, increasing to three by the third week. This approach provides structure to track progress and helps maintain motivation as measurable improvements occur over time (Young et al., 2023).

Journal to Reflect and Plan

Dedicating time each day or week to journal about experiences with new habits provides teachers with a record of their efforts. Write down what worked well and what could be improved, then set intentions for the next steps. For example, a reflection might be "Today, I successfully paused for wait time before calling on students, but I need to improve how I prompt follow-up questions." Journaling acts like a personal trainer for a teacher's thoughts, keeping them accountable and motivated (Pennebaker & Smyth, 2016; Schön, 1983).

Use Visual Reminders

Place sticky notes, sentence strips, or posters around the classroom or workspace in strategic locations, or set a timer on a phone to act as a cue for the habits being developed. For example, the teacher might keep a note on their desk with a reminder to "Pause and invite student ideas" or place a sign near their whiteboard prompting them to "Ask students to summarize main ideas." These visual reminders serve as gentle nudges, helping the teacher consistently focus on their goals throughout the day.

Preschool teachers who work with early childhood students with autism in Los Angeles were working hard to implement open-ended questions when they conducted read-alouds, as this was more likely to prompt student thinking and solicit more language from students. Figure 10.2 illustrates this concept in action, showing how teachers embedded visual reminders—sticky notes—directly into their read-aloud materials to model higher-order questioning. By distinguishing between closed and open prompts, this simple yet powerful visual makes the invisible habits of expert questioning visible, helping teachers internalize new practices and prompting students to think more deeply and expressively.

Figure 10.2   Sticky Notes as Visual Reminders

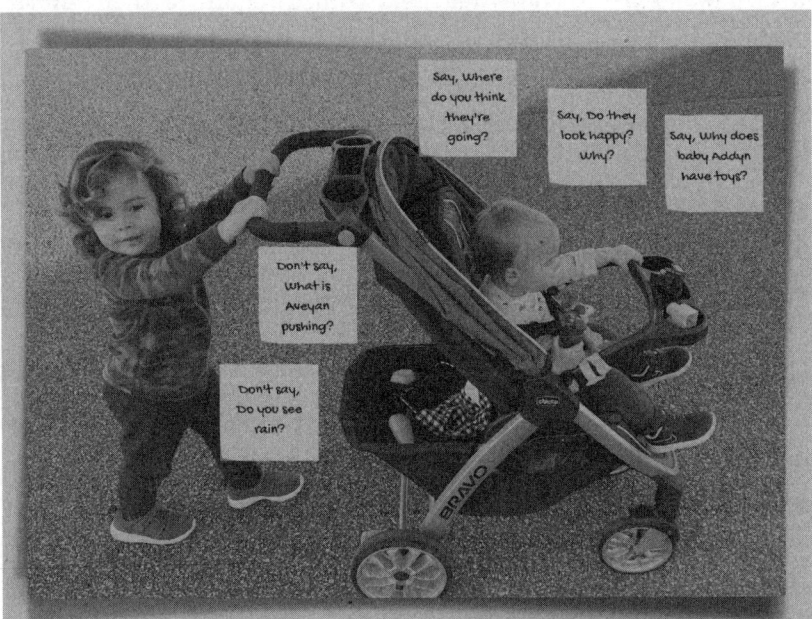

Apply the Habit Loop Framework

When the teacher notices the signals or triggers that prompt them to perform the planned behaviors, they should build routines around responding to those triggers and celebrate or acknowledge success when there is follow-through with the routine. For instance, if the cue is about how to start a lesson, the routine could involve "sharing the objective and engaging students in a brief discussion at the beginning of each lesson." The reward might be "noticing higher student engagement." This type of process—a simple cue (lesson plan note) and a quick reward (increased engagement)—often transforms abstract goals into concrete, repeatable actions (Clear, 2018).

Establish Accountability Partnerships

Routinely pairing with a colleague or friend to review progress on new habits strengthens personal accountability. Teachers could plan weekly meetings to touch base and share updates on their journeys. Having someone else involved in personal progress creates mutual motivation, similar to working out with a friend—it's much harder to skip a commitment when another person is relying on the interaction (Hwang et al., 2020).

Articulate and Share Goals

Clearly stating goals and intentions aloud or in writing significantly increases the likelihood of the teacher achieving their objectives. For example, say something like "Today, I'll make an effort to involve my quieter students more" or write a reminder such as "This week, I'll practice giving students specific, positive praise every day." Sharing these intentions with a friend, colleague, or even your students can increase motivation and help the teacher stay committed. Research by Epton and colleagues (2017) shows that clearly defined goals, particularly when paired with tracking progress and getting feedback, greatly boost the chances of achieving your desired behaviors and results. Articulating goals provides clarity and sets the tone for intentional and focused action, similar to athletes psyching themselves up before a big game.

Long-Term, High-Prep Strategies

Engage in Microteaching

Microteaching involves a teacher asking a trusted colleague, instructional coach, or friend to sit in on a class or watch a recording of their teaching. The teacher gives the observer clear points to pay attention to, such as how long they wait after asking questions or how evenly they manage student participation. Although general peer coaching has shown minimal impact on student academic outcomes, Hattie (2023) identified microteaching—a form of teacher learning involving recorded lessons and targeted discussions about these recordings—as having a substantial positive effect on student achievement (effect size = 1.01).

Likewise, microcoaching involves filming the teacher's lesson or short instructional activity, then discussing the video afterward with a colleague or coach to examine specific aspects of their teaching (Young et al., 2023). Getting feedback from someone else can offer fresh insights and highlight small details that might be overlooked when reflecting on teaching alone. Think of it like having a spotter at the gym: they see the details that might be missed and help elevate a practice to the next level.

New strategies only matter when they move from good intentions to consistent practice. Follow-through is the bridge between knowing and doing: the space where professional growth takes root. Whether the teacher relies on digital reminders, reflective journaling, or accountability partners, the goal is to make improvement visible and sustainable rather than situational. Each small act of consistency—pausing for feedback, revisiting a new habit, or refining a lesson—builds momentum toward mastery. Over time, those steady, intentional choices transform daily routines into a professional rhythm of reflection, adaptation, and progress. In the end, follow-through isn't about perfection; it's about persistence—the hallmark of truly effective teaching.

References

Abdallah, L. S., & Ali, F. N. K. (2023). Effect of digital detox program on electronic screen syndrome among preparatory school students. *Nursing Open, 10*(4).

Aguilar, E. (2018). *Onward: Cultivating emotional resilience in educators.* Jossey-Bass.

Aguilar, E. (2024). *Arise: The art of transformational coaching.* Jossey-Bass.

Almarode, J. T., Fisher, D., Thunder, K., & Frey, N. (2021). *The success criteria playbook: A hands-on guide to making learning visible and measurable.* Corwin.

American Psychological Association. (2025). *Inclusive language guidelines.* https://www.apa.org/about/apa/equity-diversity-inclusion/language-guidelines

Anderson, E., & Buchko, K. J. (2016). Giving negative feedback to millennials. *Management Research Review, 39*(6), 692–705.

Archer, A. L. (2015). *Explicit vocabulary instruction: Words for everyone* [DVD series]. Ancora.

Archer, A. L., & Hughes, C. A. (2011). *Explicit instruction: Effective and efficient teaching.* Guilford.

Bailey, R. A. (2021). *Conscious discipline: Building resilient classrooms* (Expanded & Updated ed.). Loving Guidance.

Beck, I. L., McKeown, M. G., & Kucan, L. (2013). *Bringing words to life: Robust vocabulary instruction* (2nd ed.). Guilford.

Bicksler, W. H. (2022). The devil's advocate role in asynchronous online discussions. *Issues in Educational Research, 32,* 632–649. https://www.iier.org.au/iier32/bicksler.pdf

Biggs, J., Tang, C., & Kennedy, G. (2022). *Teaching for quality learning at university* (5th ed.). Open University Press.

Bilmes, J. (2012). *Beyond behavior management: The six life skills children need* (2nd ed.). Redleaf.

Bocchino, R. (1999). *Emotional literacy: To be a different kind of smart.* Corwin.

Boonstra, L. (2025). *Prompt engineering.* Google. https://gptaiflow.com/assets/files/2025-01-18-pdf-1-TechAI-Goolge-whitepaper_Prompt%20Engineering_v4-af36d-cc7a49bb7269a58b1c9b89a8ae1.pdf

Borrello, V. (2023). *The role of parents in schools.* National Association for Family, School, and Community Engagement. https://nafsce.org

Briggs, T. H. (1928). Sarcasm. *School Review, 36*(9), 685–695.

Brown, B. (2017). *Braving the wilderness: The quest for true belonging and the courage to stand alone.* Random House.

Burns, M. (2023). *EdTech essentials: 12 strategies for every classroom in the age of AI.* ASCD.

Burns, M. (2024). *EdTech essentials: 12 strategies for every classroom in the age of AI* (2nd ed.). ASCD.

Busch, L. (2016). Beyond the genius bar: Cultivating leadership with a student-led tech team. *EdSurge.* https://www.edsurge.com/news/2016-07-17-beyond-the-genius-bar-cultivating-leadership-with-a-student-led-tech-team

Butler, J. (2022). *Gender trouble: Feminism and the subversion of identity* (3rd ed.). Routledge.

Canvas Study. (2022). *2022 Study from Canvas: Research and trends.* Hanover Research. https://www.hanoverresearch.com/reports-and-briefs/k-12-education/2022-trends-in-k-12-education

Center on Positive Behavioral Interventions and Supports (PBIS). (2022). *Tier 3 comprehensive functional behavior assessment (FBA) guide.* https://www.pbis.org/resource/tier-3-comprehensive-functional-behavior-assessment-fba-guide

Chrispeels, J. (1996). Effective schools and home-school-community partnership roles: A framework for parent involvement. *School Effectiveness and School Improvement, 7*(4), 297–323.

Clear, J. (2018). *Atomic habits: An easy & proven way to build good habits & break bad ones.* Avery.

Common Sense Media. (2024). https://www.commonsensemedia.org

Covey, S. R. (2020). *The 7 habits of highly effective people: 30th anniversary edition.* Simon & Schuster.

Csikszentmihalyi, M. (2013). *Creativity: Flow and the psychology of discovery and invention.* Harper Perennial Modern Classics.

Culatta, R. (2023). Transformational learning principles: Rethinking the experience of school. *Educational Leadership, 80*(6). https://www.ascd.org/el/articles/transformational-learning-principles-rethinking-the-experience-of-school

Darling-Hammond, L., & Hyler, M. E. (2023). *Preparing teachers for deeper learning.* Harvard Education Press.

Derek Bok Center for Teaching and Learning. (2024). *Hit the ground running: A handbook for new teaching fellows.* Harvard University.

Digital Wellness Lab. (2022). *Adolescent media use: Attitudes, effects, and online experiences.* Boston Children's Hospital. https://digitalwellnesslab.org/wp-content/uploads/Pulse-Survey_Adolescent-Attitudes-Effects-and-Experiences.pdf

Digital Wellness Lab. (2024). Boston Children's Hospital. https://digitalwellnesslab.org

Doan, S., Steiner, E. D., & Pandey, R. (2024). *Teacher well-being and intentions to leave in 2024: Findings from the 2024 State of the American Teacher Survey.* RAND. https://www.rand.org/t/RRA1108-12

Dweck, C. S. (2016). *Mindset: The new psychology of success* (Updated ed.). Random House.

Economides, M., Martman, J., Bell, M. J., & Sanderson, B. (2018). Improvements in stress, affect, and irritability following brief use of a mindfulness-based smartphone app: A randomized controlled trial. *Mindfulness, 9*(5), 1584–1593.

Educators for Excellence. (2024). *Voices from the classroom: A survey of America's educators.* Author.

Epstein, J. L., Sanders, M. G., Sheldon, S. B., Simon, B. S., Salinas, K. C., Jansorn, N. R., Van Voorhis, F. L., Martin, C. S., Thomas, B. G., Greenfield, M. D., Hutchins, D. J., & Williams, K. J. (2018). *School, family, and community partnerships: Your handbook for action* (4th ed.). Corwin.

Epstein, J. L., & Sheldon, S. B. (2023). *School, family, and community partnerships: Preparing educators and improving schools* (3rd ed.). Routledge.

Epton, T., Currie, S., & Armitage, C. J. (2017). Unique effects of setting goals on behavior change: Systematic review and meta-analysis. *Journal of Consulting and Clinical Psychology, 85*(12), 1182–1198.

Feldman, J. (2023). *Grading for equity: What it is, why it matters, and how it can transform schools and classrooms* (2nd ed.). Corwin.

Flamboyan Foundation. (2012). Academic parent teacher team meeting, Stanton Elementary School [Video]. www.youtube.com/watch?v=1YNsWrFiYfY&list=UUvEdSQawiMKMU-muuc1j0YA&index=3&feature=plc

Flanigan, A. E., Wheeler, J., Colliot, T., Lu, J., & Kiewra, K. A. (2024). Typed versus handwritten lecture notes and college student achievement: A meta-analysis. *Educational Psychology Review, 36*(3), Article 78.

Gabriel, F., Marrone, R., Van Sebille, Y., Kovanovic, V., & de Laat, M. (2022). Digital education strategies around the world: Practices and policies. *Irish Educational Studies, 41*(1), 85–106.

Gay, G. (2022). *Culturally responsive teaching: Theory, research, and practice* (4th ed.). Teachers College Press.

Gilliam, W. S., Maupin, A. N., Reyes, C. R., Accavitti, M., & Shic, F. (2016). *Do early educators' implicit biases regarding sex and race relate to behavior expectations and recommendations of preschool expulsions and suspensions?* Yale University Child Study Center. https://search.issuelab.org/resources/36464/36464.pdf

Goldberg, S. B., Tucker, R. P., Greene, P. A., Davidson, R. J., Wampold, B. E., Kearney, D. J., & Simpson, T. L. (2018). Mindfulness-based interventions for psychiatric disorders: A systematic review and meta-analysis. *Clinical Psychology Review, 59*, 52–60.

Graff, G., & Birkenstein, C. (2024). *They say/I say: The moves that matter in academic writing* (6th ed.). Norton.

Gray, C. (2015). *The new social story book: Revised and expanded 15th anniversary edition.* Future Horizons.

Groshell, Z. (2024). *Just tell them: The power of explanations and explicit teaching.* John Catt Educational.

Hammond, Z. (2015). *Culturally responsive teaching and the brain: Promoting authentic engagement and rigor among culturally and linguistically diverse students.* Corwin.

Hammond, Z. (2025). *Rebuilding students' learning power: Teaching for instructional equity and cognitive justice.* Corwin.

Hari Rajan, M., Herbert, C., & Polly, P. (2024). Disrupted student engagement and motivation: Observations from online and face-to-face university learning environments. *Frontiers in Education, 8.*

Hattie, J. (2023). *Visible learning: The sequel: A synthesis of over 2,100 meta-analyses relating to achievement.* Routledge.

Hattie, J. (2024). *Global research database.* Corwin Visible Learning Plus. https://www.visiblelearningmetax.com/Influences

Hattie, J., & Clarke, S. (2019). *Visible learning: Feedback.* Routledge.

Honsinger, C., & Brown, M. H. (2019). Preparing trauma-sensitive teachers: Strategies for teacher educators. *Teacher Educators' Journal, 12*, 129–152.

Hughes, C. A., Riccomini, P. J., & Dexter, C. A. (2022). Use explicit instruction. In M. T. Brownell, B. L. Billingsley, M. T. McLeskey, & D. J. Sindelar (Eds.), *High-leverage practices for inclusive classrooms* (2nd ed.) (pp. 235–264). Routledge.

Hwang, T. J., Rabheru, K., Peisah, C., Reichman, W., & Ikeda, M. (2020). Loneliness and social isolation during the COVID-19 pandemic. *International Psychogeriatrics, 32*(10), 1217–1220.

International Olympic Committee. (2024, January 25). *Celebrating full gender parity on the field of play at Paris 2024*. https://olympics.com/ioc/news/genderequalolympics-celebrating-full-gender-parity-on-the-field-of-play-at-paris-2024

Jackson, N. (2022). *Teachers' knowledge and practice: The role of secondary school students in technology integration*. (Unpublished thesis). Monash University.

Jensen, E. (2019). *Engaging students with poverty in mind: Practical strategies for raising achievement*. ASCD.

Johnson, B. (2018). *Teaching students to dig deeper: Ten essential skills for college and career readiness* (2nd ed.). Routledge.

Kabat-Zinn, J. (1990). *Full catastrophe living: Using the wisdom of your body and mind to face stress, pain, and illness*. Bantam.

Khalifa, M. (2023). *Culturally responsive school leadership*. Harvard Education Press.

Kounin, J. S. (1970). *Discipline and group management in classrooms*. Holt, Rinehart & Winston.

Kraft, M. A., & Papay, J. P. (2020). Can professional environments in schools promote teacher development? Explaining heterogeneity in returns to teaching experience. *Educational Evaluation and Policy Analysis, 42*(4), 617–645.

Laird, D. A. (1923). How the high school student responds to different incentives to work. *The Pedagogical Seminary, 30*(4), 357–365.

Lemov, D. (2021). *Teach like a champion 3.0: 63 techniques that put students on the path to college*. Jossey-Bass.

Lemov, D., Lewis, H., Williams, D., & Frazier, D. (2022). *Reconnect: Building school culture for meaning, purpose, and belonging*. Jossey-Bass/Wiley.

Little, J. W. (1993). Teachers' professional development in a climate of reform. *Educational Researcher, 22*(7), 37–47.

Marovah, T., & Mutanga, O. (2023). Decolonising participatory research: Can *Ubuntu* philosophy contribute something? *International Journal of Social Research Methodology, 27*(5), 501–516.

McKeown, M. G. (2019). Effective vocabulary instruction fosters knowing words, using words, and understanding how words work. *Language, Speech, and Hearing Services in Schools, 50*(4), 466–476.

McLeskey, J., Barringer, M.-D., Billingsley, B., Brownell, M. T., Jackson, D., Kennedy, M., ... & Ziegler, D. (2017). *High-leverage practices in special education*. Council for Exceptional Children & CEEDAR Center. https://highleveragepractices.org

Miller, J. C., & Krizan, Z. (2016). Walking facilitates positive affect (even when expecting the opposite). *Emotion, 16*(5), 775–785.

Morgan, A., & Kuhn, M. R. (2023). A 20-year guided reading research synthesis: Examining student data. *Literacy Research and Instruction, 63*(2), 1–24.

Nagoski, E., & Nagoski, A. (2019). *Burnout: The secret to unlocking the stress cycle*. Ballantine.

National Center for Education Statistics (NCES). (2023). *Report on the condition of education 2023* (NCES 2023-144). U.S. Department of Education. https://nces.ed.gov/pubsearch/pubsinfo.asp?pubid=2023144

Neff, K. D. (2023). Self-compassion: Theory, method, research, and intervention. *Annual Review of Psychology, 74*(1), 193–218.

Nguyen, M. H., Gruber, J., Marler, W., Hunsaker, A., Fuchs, J., & Hargittai, E. (2022). Staying connected while physically apart: Digital communication when face-to-face interactions are limited. *New Media & Society, 24*(9), 2046–2067.

Nicholson, J., Shimpi Driscoll, P., Kurtz, J., Márquez, D., & Wesley, L. (2019). *Culturally responsive self-care practices for early childhood educators*. Routledge.

Nieto, S. (2022). *Affirming diversity: The sociopolitical context of multicultural education* (7th ed.). Pearson.

Nieuwhof, C. (2021). *At your best: How to get time, energy, and priorities working in your favor*. WaterBrook.

Noddings, N. (2013). *Caring: A relational approach to ethics and moral education* (2nd ed.). University of California Press.

Okonofua, J. A., & Eberhardt, J. L. (2015). Two strikes: Race and the disciplining of young students. *Psychological Science, 26*(5), 617–624.

Paredes, M. C. (2010). *Parent involvement as an instructional strategy: Academic parent-teacher teams* (Unpublished doctoral dissertation). Arizona State University, Tempe, AZ.

Pauk, W., & Owens, R. J. Q. (2013). *How to study in college* (11th ed.). Cengage Learning.

Pennebaker, J. W. (1997). Writing about emotional experiences as a therapeutic process. *Psychological Science, 8*(3), 162–166.

Pennebaker, J. W., & Smyth, J. M. (2016). *Opening up by writing it down: How expressive writing improves health and eases emotional pain* (3rd ed.). Guilford.

Pew Research Center. (2023). *Mental health and the pandemic: What U.S. surveys have found*. https://www.pewresearch.org/short-reads/2023/03/02/mental-health-and-the-pandemic-what-u-s-surveys-have-found

Pew Research Center. (2024). *What it's like to be a teacher in America today*. https://www.pewresearch.org/social-trends/2024/04/04/whats-it-like-to-be-a-teacher-in-america-today

Raave, D. K., Saks, K., Pedaste, M., & Roa, E. R. (2024). How and why teachers use technology: Distinct integration practices in K–12 education. *Education Sciences, 14*(12), 1301.

RAND. (2024). *Social and emotional learning in U.S. schools: Findings from CASEL's Nationwide Policy Scan and the American Teacher Panel and American School Leader Panel Surveys*. Author. https://www.rand.org/pubs/research_reports/RRA1822-2.html

Ratey, J. J., & Manning, R. (2018). *Go wild: Eat fat, run free, be social, and follow evolution's other rules for total health and well-being*. Little, Brown.

Resnick, M. (2018). *Lifelong kindergarten: Cultivating creativity through projects, passion, peers, and play*. MIT Press.

Ritchhart, R., & Church, M. (2020). *The power of making thinking visible: Practices to engage and empower all learners*. Jossey-Bass.

Roth, K., & Dabrowski, J. (2023). *Interactive writing across grades: A small practice with big results*. Corwin.

Ryan, C. L., & Hermann-Wilmarth, J. M. (2022). *Reading the rainbow: LGBTQ-inclusive literacy instruction in the elementary classroom*. Teachers College Press.

Saphier, J., Haley Speca, M., & Gower, R. R. (2025). *The skillful teacher: Building your teaching skills* (8th ed.). Research for Better Teaching.

Sarason, I. G., Sarason, B. R., & Pierce, G. R. (1990). *Social support: An interactional view*. Wiley.

Schön, D. A. (1983). *The reflective practitioner: How professionals think in action.* Basic Books.

Scratch Foundation. (2024). Scratch learning resources. https://scratch.mit.edu/ideas

Sensoy, Ö., & DiAngelo, R. (2022). *Is everyone really equal? An introduction to key concepts in social justice education* (3rd ed.). Teachers College Press.

Serravallo, J. (2023). *The reading strategies book 2.0: Your research-based guide to developing skilled readers.* Heinemann.

Shockley, K. M., Clark, M. A., Dodd, H., & King, E. B. (2021). Work–family strategies during COVID-19: Examining gender dynamics among dual-earner couples with young children. *Journal of Applied Psychology, 106*(1), 15–28.

Skoog-Hoffman, A., Miller, A. A., Plate, R. C., Meyers, D. C., Tucker, A. S., Meyers, G., Diliberti, M. K., Schwartz, H. L., Kuhfeld, M., Jagers, R. J., Steele, L., & Schlund, J. (2024). *Social and emotional learning in U.S. schools.* RAND. https://www.rand.org/pubs/research_reports/RRA1822-2.html

Sprick, R. (2021). *Discipline in the secondary classroom: A positive approach to behavior management* (4th ed.). Ancora.

Sprick, R. S., Garrison, M., & Howard, L. M. (2021). *CHAMPs: A proactive and positive approach to classroom management* (3rd ed.). Ancora.

Sue, D. W., & Sue, D. (2023). *Counseling the culturally diverse: Theory and practice* (9th ed.). Wiley.

Thai, Y. C., Sim, D., McCaffrey, T. A., Ramadas, A., Malini, H., & Watterson, J. L. (2023). A scoping review of digital workplace wellness interventions in low- and middle-income countries. *PLoS ONE, 18*(2): e0282118.

Thomas, E. E. (2022). *The dark fantastic: Race and the imagination from* Harry Potter *to* The Hunger Games. NYU Press.

Tomlinson, C. A. (2017). *How to differentiate instruction in academically diverse classrooms* (3rd ed.). ASCD.

United Nations Educational, Scientific and Cultural Organization (UNESCO). (2023). *Global Education Monitoring Report 2023: Technology in education—A tool on whose terms?* Author. https://gem-report-2023.unesco.org

Vanderbilt University Center for Teaching. (2025). *Difficult dialogues.* https://derekbruff.org/vanderbilt-cft-teaching-guides-archive/difficult-dialogues

Van der Kolk, B. (2014). *The body keeps the score: Brain, mind, and body in the healing of trauma.* Penguin.

Vaughn, S. R., Bos, C. S., & Schumm, J. S. (2014). *Teaching students who are exceptional, diverse, and at risk in the general education classroom* (6th ed.). Pearson.

Versy. (2025). *A complete Oxford debate guide by today's experts.* Versy Blog. https://www.versytalks.com/blog/a-complete-oxford-debate-guide-by-today-s-experts

Vygotsky, L. S. (1978). *Mind in society: The development of higher psychological processes.* Harvard University Press.

Wang, C., & Le, H. (2022). The more, the merrier? Roles of device–student ratio in collaborative inquiries and its interactions with external scripts and task complexity. *Journal of Educational Computing Research, 59*(8), 1517–1542.

Waterson, J. (2024). The Community Resiliency Model (CRM) applied to teacher's well-being. https://core.ac.uk/download/603654299.pdf

Watson, E., & Busch, B. (2021). *The science of learning: 99 studies that every teacher needs to know.* Routledge.

WebbAlign. (2024). Depth of Knowledge (DoK) explained. https://www.webbalign.org/about/dok-explained

WestEd. (2016a). Academic Parent Teacher Teams training presented to Goodland Elementary School staff in Racine, WI [Workshop materials].

WestEd. (2016b). Coach for Success and Teach for Success training presented to Goodland Elementary School staff in Racine, WI [Workshop materials].

White, M. P., Elliott, L. R., Grellier, J., Wheeler, B. W., Bone, A., Depledge, M. H., & Fleming, L. E. (2023). Nature-based biopsychosocial resilience: An integrative conceptual framework. *Environmental Research, 181,* 313–328.

Will, M. (2019). How can teachers bounce back from failure? *Education Week.* https://www.edweek.org/teaching-learning/how-can-teachers-bounce-back-from-failure/2019/05

Xu, L., & Carless, D. (2021). Aligning assessment with the needs of work-integrated learning: The importance of ensuring reflective practice. *Assessment & Evaluation in Higher Education, 46*(3), 454–467.

Yosso, T. J., & Solórzano, D. G. (2022). *Critical race counterstories along the Chicana/Chicano educational pipeline.* Routledge.

Young, A. K. (2025). *Confident classroom management moves (QuickWins! Strategy Cards).* ASCD.

Young, A. K., Julien, A. B., & Osborne, T. (2023). *The instructional coaching handbook: 200+ troubleshooting strategies for success.* ASCD.

Young, A. K., & Osborne, T. (2023). *Training design, delivery, & diplomacy: An educator's guide.* ASCD.

Index

The letter *f* following a page locator denotes a figure.

About the Authors

A. Keith Young is an education coach, trainer, and writer. Keith was born and raised in the foothills of the Appalachian Mountains of northern Alabama. He studied to be an English teacher. After a short stint at seminary, he pivoted to teaching secondary students English and math for the U.S. government in Germany. In his first years of teaching, he developed a knack for leading and training colleagues. In addition, he was immersed in training and coaching from prominent educational leaders, including Jon Saphier, Louise Thomson, Ernie Stokowski, Robby Champion, Rick DuFour, and Robert Garmston. Eventually, Keith shifted full-time to training teachers and leading school improvement efforts at the school district level. Later, he became a principal, leading school turnaround work and regularly increasing student outcomes by double digits in Colorado, Puerto Rico, and Arizona. Along the way, Keith picked up several advanced education degrees.

Nowadays, Keith trains and coaches administrators, school leadership teams, and teacher coaches. As a trainer, he maintains a progressive philosophy and a teaching style that embraces the best of constructivism and direct instruction. As a coach, he's known for "telling it like it is" and using a blended coaching model. The schools Keith coaches across the United States and internationally produce significant increases in student outcomes, both academically and affectively.

**Angela Bell Julien** owns and manages Angela Bell Julien Publications & Consulting. She provides school leaders and teachers with practical implementation strategies in site leadership, instructional improvement, strategic cycles of inquiry for systemic improvement, and relationship building.

Angela was born in Phoenix, Arizona. She never planned on becoming a teacher, but her college majors in English and theater led her to the high school classroom, where she was profoundly changed by encounters with students who were lost in the system. Angela followed the work of William Glasser, Ted Sizer, Jon Saphier, Bruce Wellman, and others and quickly became a leader of her peers as department chair, peer evaluator, assistant principal for curriculum and instruction, and high school principal. All told, she spent close to 35 years working in high schools. Intrigued by the small learning communities movement, she molded the process into a pathway to provide equity, decrease dropout rates, and increase post–high school success for all students.

From 2008 to 2021, Angela served as a school and district improvement facilitator for WestEd, providing training, professional development, and technical assistance to support leadership, differentiated instruction, writing instruction, and student achievement improvement efforts for K–12 schools in Hawaii, Arizona, California, Nevada, Maryland, and Colorado. Angela also paints and writes poetry; she has three published books of illustrated poetry and prompted journals.

 **Tamarra Osborne** is a project manager, trainer, and coach with WestEd, a national nonprofit in San Francisco, California. Born and raised in Oakland, California, she's one of five siblings and a first-generation college graduate. Deciding to stay close to a tight-knit family, she attended California State University in Sacramento. Tamarra earned a degree in early childhood education, realizing a dream that began at age 16 when she started working with preschoolers for Oakland's Parks and Recreation Department. After a brief period teaching English in Japan, she launched her teacher leadership and early care career.

Tamarra's philosophy of early education favors students learning through experiences and using play to learn academics. After 10 years directing an innovative childcare center in California, Tamarra took her expertise to WestEd. At WestEd, she serves as the project manager for the Desired Results Training and Technical Assistance Project, which provides a groundbreaking statewide observational assessment of young learners.

Tamarra is known as an effervescent trainer and technical coach who sees the heart of a problem and provides sensible, warm-hearted solutions. Tamarra has a knack for technology proficiency and delivers training and coaching in multiple U.S. states, as well as in China. Her training topics include formative assessment, curriculum development, presentation skills, implicit bias, and educational technology. Tamarra is proud to be published in *Young Children* magazine from the National Association for the Education of Young Children.

Judith Mendoza-Jiménez is a first-generation U.S. immigrant, bilingual special educator, and educational leader dedicated to supporting diverse learners. After immigrating from Mexico at age 10, she earned advanced degrees in special education from the University of Arizona and in educational leadership from Northern Arizona University, all while steadily moving up the ranks from special education teacher to assistant principal to high school principal.

Judith now serves as the director of student services for the Nogales Unified School District, where she leads the development of inclusive instructional and behavioral support systems. Judith is a published author in *The Learning Professional*. Married for 21 years, she enjoys life with her husband and their two beloved fur babies.